PRAISE F

BEYOND OUR CONTROL

"Michael and Lauren McAfee have walked through trials that could have broken them, but instead they felt their way to Jesus. They will help you do the same. If you or someone you know is walking through a season of grief, this is the book you need."

—**Jennie Allen**, *New York Times* bestselling author of *Find Your People* and *Get Out of Your Head* and founder and visionary of IF:Gathering

"Lots of us in our scariest and darkest moments want to talk to someone who 'gets it,' someone who's been where we are and who can point us to life on the other side of the grief. Lauren and Michael McAfee wisely guide us through what it's like to live through confusing or sorrow-filled times without losing heart. If you're hurting, or if you love someone who is, this book is here for you, maybe at exactly the right time."

—**Russell Moore**, editor in chief of Christianity Today

"If you've ever been looking for a path for developing greater trust in God, Michael and Lauren have provided the resource for you in this book. As they walk through their own struggles, they share the invaluable lessons they've learned to find deeper connection with God on the other side of their pain."

—**Nick Vujicic**, evangelist, author, and entrepreneur

"Michael and Lauren McAfee offer real and insightful encouragement to those who find themselves in seasons of anxiety, loss, and disappointment. They draw from personal pain and deep reliance on the Lord through each trial. We recommend this book to anyone whose life hasn't turned out like they thought it would."

—**Matt and Lauren Chandler**, pastor, author, and speaker; worship leader, author, and speaker

"This book is a gem. We were captivated by Michael and Lauren's poignant personal story of waiting, adoption, and loss. They wrestled and held on to the goodness of God amidst their grief. They encourage readers that God is able to do something immeasurably greater than we can imagine through the pain. We strongly recommend this book for anyone wrestling to make sense of suffering and powerlessness in light of the cross."

—**Timothy and Joyce Dalrymple**, president and CEO of Christianity Today; author and founder of Refuge for Strength

"Michael and Lauren's story is utterly gripping. Their willingness to talk so openly about the struggles they have faced with childlessness, adoption, and loss is a gift to others. Their story of encounters with God through these trials is a challenge and encouragement to us all."

—**Peter J. Williams**, PhD, principal and CEO of Tyndale House, Cambridge

"This book is a thoughtful and touching resource for anyone struggling with the problem of pain and suffering. Michael and Lauren are uniquely qualified because of their own life experience. But more than that, their insights come from a deep sense of faith and a strong commitment to and love for God's Word. This book tackles some of life's most perplexing questions with honesty, grace, and wisdom."

—**Rick Thompson**, senior pastor of Council Road Baptist Church and president of Global Action

"Lauren and Michael offer their grief as a guide to anyone who has stared in the face of deep disappointment, powerless vulnerability, and unspeakable sorrow, and had the courage to ask, 'Why?' Their raw, emotional honesty, hemmed in by the soul-protecting truth of Scripture, presents the freedom of trusting the promises and power of God with all that is beyond our control."

—**Katie J. McCoy**, PhD, director of women's ministry at Texas Baptists and author of *To Be A Woman*

"Lauren and Michael combine personal experience with biblical truth to walk through their moments of deep despair, yet still find hope in the providence of God. Michael and Lauren show a pathway for relinquishing control and trusting God's higher ways. This book should be read by anyone going through a tough period or helping others through difficulty, but it is also a great reminder of God's plans and ways for all Christians."

—**Bob Doll**, chief investment officer of Crossmark Global Investments

BEYOND OUR CONTROL

LET GO OF UNMET EXPECTATIONS, OVERCOME ANXIETY, AND DISCOVER INTIMACY WITH GOD

LAUREN & MICHAEL McAFEE

An Imprint of Thomas Nelson

Beyond Our Control

Published in Nashville, Tennessee, by Nelson Books, an imprint of Thomas Nelson. Nelson Books and Thomas Nelson are registered trademarks of HarperCollins Christian Publishing, Inc.

Authors are represented by Alive Literary Agency, www.aliveliterary.com

Thomas Nelson titles may be purchased in bulk for educational, business, fundraising, or sales promotional use. For information, please email SpecialMarkets@ThomasNelson.com.

ISBN 978-1-4002-3522-3

Library of Congress Cataloging-in-Publication Data

Names: McAfee, Michael, 1987- author. | McAfee, Lauren Green, author.
Title: Beyond our control : let go of unmet expectations, overcome anxiety, and discover intimacy with God / Lauren and Michael McAfee.
Description: Nashville, Tennessee : Nelson Books, [2023] | Summary: "Realizing how little control we have over our lives can make us fearful and anxious--or it can lead to greater intimacy with God, a richer prayer life, and a joyful eternal perspective"-- Provided by publisher.
Identifiers: LCCN 2023023343 (print) | LCCN 2023023344 (ebook) | ISBN 9781400235193 (tp) | ISBN 9781400235209 (epub)
Subjects: LCSH: Christian life. | Change (Psychology)--Religious aspects--Christianity. | Presence of God.
Classification: LCC BV4599.5.C44 M39 2023 (print) | LCC BV4599.5.C44 (ebook) | DDC 248.4--dc23/eng/20230710
LC record available at https://lccn.loc.gov/2023023343
LC ebook record available at https://lccn.loc.gov/2023023344

Printed in the United States of America

24 25 26 27 28 LBC 5 4 3 2 1

For Zion,
the special girl who made us parents.
We are so lucky to have you.

And for Ezra,
though you will never remember us,
we could never forget you.

CONTENTS

FOREWORD

We've all encountered situations that are beyond our control, and as much as we try to change, solve, work around, or influence them, they can seem as immovable as a brick wall that constricts our lives. Such circumstances can involve our relationships, painful emotions, troublesome behaviors, finances, or health. And they can be mild, moderate, severe, or totally overwhelming.

We all get stuck and feel discouraged from time to time in our attempts to "control the uncontrollable," which can be debilitating. That is why Michael and Lauren's book will help you, no matter the challenges you presently face.

Lauren and Michael have written a deeply personal and instructive book from the context of their difficult experiences with adoption, infertility, and illness, and it's from this place of significant challenge that you'll come to know the authors' "insides" in an intimate way while also gaining useful insight from the biblical principles that have seen them through. Even if you have not experienced these exact hardships, you will find these pages filled with highly applicable ideas that meet you right where you are.

I met Michael and Lauren a number of years ago, before they had faced many of the circumstances they will describe in this book. Watching their gratitude for God's kindness—even in trying times—made these chapters an encouragement to read. This couple isn't offering us their aspirations for how they wish to someday live but rather their inspiration and instruction for living this way today.

Circumstances that lie beyond our control can make us feel different or even very isolated. Believing that no one else really gets what life is like for us, we keep our struggle to ourselves and detach a little more every day from people who might help if they only knew.

In those situations we need to know that someone who has been there can understand us and is willing to show us the way forward. Further, we need someone to point us toward God, "who comforts us in all our affliction, so that we may be able to comfort those who are in any affliction, with the comfort with which we ourselves are comforted by God" (2 Corinthians 1:4 ESV).

Michael and Lauren are these "someones." They have walked the hard path already and have earned the right to lead us along. Psychologists speak of the process called "identification" as a powerful tool to help bring support and strength in circumstances beyond our control. Michael and Lauren can connect in a "yes, me too" manner. As you read their journey of not being in control, you will think, *They've been there. They've earned the right to say these things. They get me.* And they do.

And then there is the encouragement of encountering a solid biblical framework for addressing the emotional and mental weight that mounts when life goes wrong. Michael and Lauren have done their theological homework in this material, a reflection of their doctoral-level training in biblical studies and ability to correctly handle "the word of truth" (2 Timothy 2:15).

Take this example from the first chapter, "Misconceptions: The Half-Lies We Like to Believe." Here Michael and Lauren address inaccurate teachings about how the world should work. For instance, when reading in Romans 12:15, which exhorts us to "Rejoice with those who rejoice, weep with those who weep," it's tempting to think, *Well, if we are to rejoice on some occasions and mourn on others, then suffering and joy must be diametrically opposed.* And if suffering and joy stand in opposition to each other, then we can't experience one while experiencing the other.

But the problem with this approach, as Michael explains, is

that if we dedicate our lives to the avoidance of suffering, we might steer clear of some pain and trouble but according to Jesus' words we will also miss joy. "In this world you will have trouble. But take heart! I have overcome the world" (John 16:33).

The clarification is helpful: when we are faced with suffering that we can't control, instead of avoiding or denying it, we are to understand that by staying focused on Jesus and all he provides we are able to take heart, to be joyful. A clear biblical principle about a key emotional truth.

Michael and Lauren also provide us with wise insight that we aren't always totally helpless and, in many ways, do have some measure of control over our situations. Sometimes when we are faced with a hardship, we think that all we can do is pray and wait. That may be true. But most of the time there are mental, emotional, behavioral, and relational choices we can make that can help the problem resolve. The authors call this "partial control" in chapter 5, which deals with powerlessness. That is an empowering reality to keep us in the balance between two extremes: being control freaks and living in what psychologists call "learned helplessness."

In this book we also have the encouragement of the authors' transformational stories. We all love a good story. Compelling narratives about real flesh-and-blood people just like us grab our attention, draw us in, and leave us changed. And because they resonate with us on both an emotional and a physical level, the stories help us make sense of the stories unfolding in our own lives.

Because Michael and Lauren express themselves so vulnerably—allowing you "in the room" as it were—you will find yourself engaged by their firsthand experience and reminded of your own path. You'll experience with them the serious hardships they've faced, including not being able to conceive a biological child; the bewildering wait they endured before finally adopting their daughter Zion; walking the scary and lonely path of a cancer diagnosis; losing their beloved son, Ezra, after a year; walking along with Lauren's sister, Lindy, and her husband, Danny, as they had to bury their hours-old child.

But over and over again Beyond Our Control brings these stories to us with a point, and the point has to do with spiritual growth. As Lauren and Michael say, this book is not a memoir. It is much more. It brings you to a God who heals and transforms that which is beyond our control.

Then there is the final encouragement, that of ultimately being pointed to Jesus.

The authors' most important goal is that this book draws us closer to Jesus, because in the ultimate analysis only an intimate walk with him can fully allow us to overcome fear with peace. "Peace I leave with you," Jesus said. "My peace I give you. I do not give to you as the world gives. Do not let your hearts be troubled and do not be afraid" (John 14:27).

Research states that one of the hallmarks of emotional health is a person's ability to simultaneously hold differing, even contradictory experiences. People who cannot tolerate negative circumstances, for example, feel that all of the joy in their life is drained by the negative. However, healthy people can hold the tension and live well with it. Lauren and Michael show us the way in our relationship with Jesus to live in a troubled world, facing uncontrollable circumstances and at the same time experiencing his peace, the peace that allows us to feel the hard things and the joy at the same time and move forward in faith.

I hope you will experience the many benefits of this book. God bless you.

John Townsend, PhD

Author of the Boundaries book series and founder of Townsend Institute and Townsend Leadership Program

INTRODUCTION

Twists and Turns

LAUREN

I'm guessing that what has brought you here, to these pages, is a kind of pain that feels paralyzing, the type of suffering that will never make sense, the aspects of life that linger just beyond your reach . . . beyond those things you think you control. I'm guessing that you're grateful for many things in life—the air you breathe, the opportunities you've been given, the moments you deeply enjoy. But you know as well as I do that even the richest, most plentiful blessings don't outweigh the burden of feeling out of control.

I'm guessing that while you may have always known that life comes with its share of hardships, it's the form those hardships take that has felt totally shocking to you.

You thought you'd struggle some. But did you really have to struggle like *this*?

You thought you'd experience some setbacks. But was it necessary to be kicked to the curb?

If I'm describing your experience, please know that you're not alone.

I get it.

I've lived it.

In fact, I'm still living it now.

True: my husband, Michael, and I have known lots of ups. So many. But during certain seasons the downs have nearly taken us out. Painful twists and turns we couldn't predict. Grappling with a total loss of control. But here's the truth: the same circumstances that ushered in our most debilitating heartaches led us to our deepest sense of joy.

WE'VE COME TO UNDERSTAND THAT EVEN IN THE MOST PAINFUL OF CIRCUMSTANCES, WE CAN EXPERIENCE RICH INTIMACY WITH GOD.

And while the circumstances that were beyond our control are surely different from the out-of-control situations you've found yourself in, I'm confident that you will find commonality in the themes that we've drawn in these chapters as we've wrestled with our misconceptions, our misunderstandings, and our beliefs about what we deserve in life. As we've wrestled with the God who is in control, we've come to understand that even in the most painful of circumstances, we can experience rich intimacy with him.

Admittedly, this doesn't remove the challenge we're up against—the struggle, the loss, the defeat. But it does provide supernatural power and courage to come to that challenge changed.

Before You Dive In

A few things before you dive in. First, I wish I could be sitting across the table from you with a cup of hot coffee in hand to hear about the situation in your life that has drawn you to this book. I'm sure it has included unexpected twists and painful turns and circumstances beyond your control. In lieu of that in-person conversation, I pray that across these pages, as you hear about the heartaches Michael and I have endured, you will come to understand that you're not alone in your struggle, that others have been where you are. I pray also that hope will be restored in your heart as you revisit what the Bible has to say about grief, about God, and about how our grief can lead us to God.

Second, I want to prepare you at the outset that Michael's and my journey centers on the topic of adoption—a complex and charged subject, given that adoption is always born in brokenness. Because families were intended to remain intact, adoption exists only because our world is not as it should be. Even the pursuit of biological reunification, which you would think would be the goal of every foster care and adoptive situation, is never as straightforward as it should be. Whatever was broken that caused a child to be placed with non-biological caregivers may persist—at least at some level—to the point where handing over that boy or girl to the family member who desires to raise that little one is a complicated event.

I say all of this to acknowledge that each adoption story is told from three distinct perspectives—an "adoption triad" that includes the point of view of the biological parents, the adoptee, and the adoptive parents. In the writing of our experience, please note that Michael and I can only speak from our perspective—that of the adoptive parents. This perspective is in no way meant to diminish the perspectives of the biological parents, which surely would differ from ours. It is also not meant to minimize the perspective of the adoptee, whose perspective deserves to be heard and validated. It is to say that we can speak only from our experience and acknowledge the importance of each side of the triad.

Finally, while this book should not be considered a memoir, Michael and I do share glimpses of our story in each chapter to demonstrate the ways in which we grasped for control in the face of circumstances that were clearly uncontrollable. At the root of our understandable reactions were errant beliefs we held, beliefs we'll lay out for you in chapter 1. I trust that seeing how our beliefs led to our assumptions and how those assumptions fueled our actions will help you assess your own life's progression and address the hard circumstances you face.

Our Story

When Michael and I married in 2009, we both were fresh-faced twenty-one-year-olds. We were students at a huge secular university, and nobody in our friend group was seriously dating, let alone contemplating marriage. But we'd known each other for fourteen years by that point and figured we'd waited long enough.

I don't know how you felt at age twenty-one, but for me, motherhood seemed like a distant box to check. If I ever were to become a mom, it would be far into the future, I hoped. I was young. My marriage was new. I have a mind for business. What was the hurry, anyway?

Four years into our marriage, I remember treating Michael to an amazing steak dinner to celebrate his twenty-fifth birthday. We absolutely could not afford that meal, but I wanted to do something special for him because I had important news to share.

I was pregnant—not with a baby but with an idea. "I think it's time we considered adoption," I said.

Michael's eyes grew very wide as a smile overtook his face.

"Really?" he said.

Yeah, really.

This was a big deal, and Michael knew it. I wasn't the type of woman who had a raging maternal instinct. I'm still not. But lately, as I explained to my husband, every time I'd been alone in my car and my thoughts had drifted to the prospect of international adoption, tears would spring to my eyes. I'd taken this as a sign that we were supposed to proceed in that direction. And while I may not have been very "motherly," I've always strived to be obedient to the Holy Spirit's promptings.

IF THIS WAS WHERE GOD WAS LEADING US, THEN WHO WAS I TO SAY NO?

If this was where God was leading us, then who was I to say no?

"Why don't we take the next forty days and pray over this decision?" Michael asked—a sensible, responsible reply from a man who has always been more mature than his years, even as the very next night he came home with the initial application—printed out and ready to sign. We knew there wouldn't be a match made overnight, but we were eager to get started in the process.

It would be nearly seven years after that delicious, overpriced dinner before one of our adoption attempts finally resulted in our becoming parents, a story you'll read in the pages to come. But if anyone has ever been worth the wait, our little girl was that one. From the moment we met this little nineteen-month-old in the Chinese adoption office, Michael and I could tell that Zion was one of the most observant and adorable little girls ever to grace this earth.

Life was good.

Our dreams were coming true.

But a nightmare would soon unfold.

After Zion had been with us for a little more than a month, Michael and I received a call that would rock us to our core. In the process of completing several routine medical checks upon entering the United States, a tumor was discovered on Zion's liver that was deemed cancerous.

During the months following her cancer diagnosis, we began writing this book—this would have been January of 2020. We thought that we'd write about our past experiences and our lessons learned—something like, *Wow, was that ever a difficult season and aren't we glad it's over now!* But the reality was that God was preparing us for an even more challenging road ahead. February of 2020 brought with it the launch of a new "faith travel" ministry called Inspire that Michael and I had been dreaming about for years, but things were brought to a screeching halt when, in mid-March, the COVID-19 pandemic shut down the world. Personally and professionally, it was an extremely disorienting season. I'm sure you can relate. Everyone was forced to reckon with the reality that so much of life is frustratingly outside our control.

Despite the setbacks of 2020, we did receive a pleasant surprise late in the year: after our adoption with Zion, we began the process of adopting again, and this time, instead of an international adoption, we pursued a domestic infant adoption. To our surprise, within a few weeks of our paperwork being finished, we received a call that a birth mother had chosen us to parent her baby boy. With great anticipation we brought home Zion's baby brother, Ezra,[1] and began learning about life with a newborn—and as a family of four.

But once again, days we took as dreamy culminated in a ridiculous nightmare for us. Ezra was in our home for twelve months, becoming more integral to our family with every day that passed.

But due to some unusual circumstances, the court ordered us to hand him over to a biological family member who had decided he wanted Ezra after all.

Shockingly, we were given only a couple of hours to explain to Zion that she would need to say goodbye to her baby brother—not just for today but for forever. It has been one year since that agonizing transition, and still today, we're deeply grieved.

Even so, we have kept engaging.

We have kept on learning.

We have kept on writing the lessons we've learned.

And while we keep thinking the toughest parts are behind us, God keeps trusting us with more pain.

Just last month, Michael and I learned that my sister's precious baby boy, Oliver, whom she carried for nearly thirty-two weeks, had lived only minutes after being born prematurely before dying in her arms.

How in the world do we make sense of all this?

How in the world do you?

We keep living.

Keep engaging.

Keep learning.

Keep hoping.

Keep trusting God with what he alone can control.

Our daughter's cancer diagnosis and difficult surgery? Those things were within God's perfect control. Our loss of our beautiful son, Ezra? That whole situation was within God's perfect control. Lindy's devastating pain as she shed tears over Oliver's deceased body? God was there, controlling it all. The years of infertility Michael and I have faced as we prayed that having biological children could also be part of our plan? Those years are within God's control—his perfect and sovereign control. At

AS THINGS FELT INCREASINGLY UNSETTLED, WE HAVE SEEN GOD COME TO US AND SETTLE OUR SOULS.

every turn, as things felt increasingly unsettled, we have seen God come to us and settle our souls. He is good, he would remind us. He is kind. He has promised to provide for us all that we need. And despite all the instincts and impulses of our human nature, it is only when we cede all control to him that we can move confidently and purposefully through the inevitable pain of life.

Moving Toward Intimacy

Let me offer up one final note before I pass the mic to my husband for a few pages: If you're a theology nerd like we are, you may have noticed that the contents of this book are laid out in a chiasm—an ancient writing structure often used in the book of Psalms in which the first and last lines complement each other, the second and second-to-last lines complement each other, the third and third-to-last complement each other, and so on, with each of the pairs pointing toward a centerpiece theme—a fulcrum. If you look at the chiasm graphically, you should see the left half of the letter *X* (Greek *chi*, pronounced "kī") forming a right-facing arrow directed at that centermost point.

The reason we structured the book in this way is twofold: first, suffering can often feel like a slow descent into agony and awfulness. Have you discovered that this is true? You're faced with impossible circumstances, and things only get worse from there!

We wanted to attend to that truth: Life gets messy. Things feel hard. We are made to deal with our own blind spots; we are made to wrestle with emotions we don't want to feel; we are made to fall flat on our face a thousand times, having nowhere to look but up.

INTIMACY WITH JESUS IS WHAT ALLOWS US TO SEE THAT THE GREATEST JOY WE'LL EVER KNOW IS BEING TOTALLY OUT OF CONTROL.

But a second thing is equally true: If we do choose to look up, we'll find comfort. We'll find healing. We'll find hope. And thus the bottom leg of the chiasm, which rebuilds all that's been lost.

The center point, as you'll notice, is intimacy with Jesus. And as we journey through these concepts together, I hope you'll keep that goal in mind. While it's the case that Michael authored some of this book's chapters and I authored others, we shared a singular, unifying motivation for every syllable we wrote: *intimacy with Jesus is the goal*. Closeness with Jesus means closeness with providence. With perspective. With righteousness. With lament. With peace.

Intimacy with Jesus is what allows us to see that the greatest joy we'll ever know is being totally out of control. For it is in that place of complete surrender that his power surges strong.

CHAPTER 1

MISCONCEPTIONS

The Half-Lies We Like to Believe

No one can act outside of God's sovereign will or against it.

—JERRY BRIDGES

MICHAEL

For many married couples, the expectation of having children is at the top of their list. Lauren and I kind of ambled toward that next step, taking our time instead of running full speed. Once we decided it was time to pursue adoption—our plan A likely motivated by Lauren growing up in a family that prioritized and practiced the process of adoption—we thought things would fall into place. Unlike a biological addition to a family, adoptions can take eighteen months to two years, sometimes even three. We were twenty-five at the time, and the math felt good. We would become parents at twenty-seven, twenty-eight years old, which seemed about right to us.

But while we had confidently chosen adoption, adoption evidently wasn't choosing us. We waited for nearly seven long years for a child through the adoption process, to no avail. In the meantime, we also turned to the biological alternative, which proved equally fruitless. As the months went by and our home remained devoid of sweet giggles and late-night wails, our hearts began to sink. Our instincts craved control. If children are a blessing from the Lord, a "reward" as Psalm 127:3 calls them, then why was this earnest desire of our hearts feeling like a curse?

Things were not going according to our plan.

You can probably relate. The greatest obstacles to discovering deep joy from intimacy with God are the lies we like to believe. True joy is found in truth. No joy is sustainable if it is based on a lie, which means that untruths are actual enemies to us—to our happiness and livelihood and peace. False beliefs distort our understanding of reality, and when we can't grasp the truth of reality, how are we supposed to live?

Lauren and I both grew up in Oklahoma, and while we love our home state enough to still live there, we've always enjoyed traveling—especially to big cities. So, when there was an opportunity to move from Oklahoma to New York City early in our marriage, we jumped at the chance and quickly settled into the Upper West Side of Manhattan.

THE GREATEST OBSTACLES TO DISCOVERING DEEP JOY FROM INTIMACY WITH GOD ARE THE LIES WE LIKE TO BELIEVE.

The opportunity had become apparent to Lauren and me after we realized that in our work with Museum of the Bible the year prior, we'd been on the road forty-six of the fifty-two weeks. *Forty-six.* Who cared where we lived? We lived in airports, anyway. Furthermore, with my boss based in Kansas City and Lauren's boss in Nashville, it was clear the museum was more concerned about our performance than where we established our home base. It was a quick nine months that we called New York home, but we loved every minute of our time there.

I remember like it was yesterday walking the bustling streets, staring skyward and feeling awed by the jungle of tall buildings rising around us. It seemed there was always construction going on with new building projects stretching up to the Manhattan sky. Each of those skyscrapers had to have a deep foundation to soar to such heights, to remain standing during stiff winds and storms, to persist against the force of gravity that sought to bear down on them. I think you and I require similar grounding, a similar sturdiness to thrive and persist. The way I see it, our lives will only reach the heights of joy insomuch as we have dug a deep foundation of truth. More truth equals more potential for joy. Less truth equals less potential for joy—and for wisdom and peace and hope and all the rest.

The challenge, then, is how to get lots of truth.

What I've come to understand is that most people don't intentionally believe lies. Nobody sets out to become foolish, to be manipulated, to be hooked on false claims. What happens instead is that they settle for half-truths and then build their lives on those.

These are the half-truths we love.

Jesus taught that you and I can choose to build our lives on the sand and watch as a storm destroys everything, or we can build our lives on the rock so that we have a solid foundation to stand on when the storms around us rage. No one sets out to build his life on sand, even as many justify living on the spiritual equivalent of Rockaway Beach by claiming that the foundation is secure enough.

NOBODY SETS OUT TO BE HOOKED ON FALSE CLAIMS. INSTEAD THEY SETTLE FOR HALF-TRUTHS AND BUILD THEIR LIVES ON THOSE.

In the Western world today, the church has largely embraced the half-truth that God's primary function is to intervene in our lives such that our suffering is eased, our stress is calmed, and our success is pretty much ensured. This comes in varying degrees of absurdity, from the blazing televangelists promising financial provision for any person who supports their ministry, all the way down to the more subtle foolishness that if we live a good Christian life, God will reward us in this life with a mostly pain-free, prosperous existence. The Enemy need not concern himself with radically derailing our walk with God if he can lure us just far enough away that we remain unaware we have strayed ever so slightly from the narrow path.

As far as our material possessions, Philippians 4:19 says, "And my God will meet all your needs according to the riches of his glory in Christ Jesus." Deuteronomy 8:18 shows that God gives us the ability to become rich while also telling us this: "But remember the LORD your God, for it is he who gives you the ability to produce wealth, and so confirms his covenant, which he swore to your ancestors, as it is today." And Jesus himself said he came so that we may have the abundant life in John 10:10: "The thief comes only to steal and kill and destroy; I have come that they may have life, and have it to the full." How much clearer can it get, right? The Bible tells us that God's plan is for us to be prosperous and abundant in wealth.

Doesn't it?

This is where things get sticky.

It's tempting to use portions of Scripture to prove that prosperity is what God intends for our lives, even twisting ever so slightly the other promises of God so that this prosperity extends beyond money and possessions to include family as well. Consider some of the passages in Scripture that speak about family. We are assured this in Proverbs 22:6: "Start children off on the way they should go, and even when they are old they will not turn from it." And more than children, grandchildren are like a crown for grandparents: "Grandchildren are the crown of the aged, and the glory of children is their fathers" (Proverbs 17:6 ESV).

Yes, we can look at Scripture and see God's promise for success across the pages. Referring to those who walk with God and who delight in the Scriptures, Psalm 1:3 says, "Whatever they do prospers." Psalm 37:3–4 adds, "Take delight in the LORD, and he will give you the desires of your heart." Finally we are to "ask and it will be given to you; seek and you will find; knock and the door will be opened to you. For everyone who asks receives; the one who seeks finds; and to the one who knocks, the door will be opened" (Matthew 7:7–8).

A few verses later we read, "If you, then, though you are evil, know how to give good gifts to your children, how much more will your Father in heaven give good gifts to those who ask him!" (v. 11).

If this is what the Bible says, then why is life so unbearably painful at times? The reality is, it's an easy mistake to correctly quote a passage of Scripture while misapplying it such that God's truth is lost in a lie. Consider when Christ was tempted in the desert by Satan, Satan was directly quoting the words of Scripture. The devil was lying while quoting truth. These half-truths can warp our understanding of how God views our circumstances, our families, and our success. The late Anglican theologian J. I. Packer famously quipped that "a half-truth masquerading as a whole truth becomes a complete untruth."[1]

When I was a kid, my belief in a half understanding of truth cost me some cold, hard cash at VBS one summer. VBS was a half-day camp for elementary kids at our church that was like a supercharged week of Sunday school taking place Monday through Friday. The experience included an opportunity for participants to gather financial support for global missions, and Lauren and I both attended and remember learning about Christians who traveled to the other side of the world to share the good news of the gospel, and we were encouraged to give sacrificially to support those missionaries' work.

After being encouraged to give financially in support of missions, I poured out all the money from my little safe, counting nearly one hundred dollars in all. Not bad for a ten-year-old, I figured. I then proceeded to give every dollar to that VBS offering, and truly, it seemed to pay off. Those of us who donated money that week collectively raised more than one thousand bucks, and our reward for hitting our collective goal was watching our senior pastor eat his least favorite food: pickled okra.

That part wasn't such a big deal, but get this: The following week was my family's scheduled vacation, but it ended up being canceled. In lieu of the trip, my parents decided to give my little brother, Bear, and me each a sum of money to spend throughout the summer on whatever we wanted. The amount? One hundred dollars exactly.

I distinctly recall thinking that this must be what Jesus meant in saying, "Give, and it will be given to you. A good measure, pressed down, shaken together and running over, will be poured into your lap. For with the measure you use, it will be measured to you" (Luke 6:38). Eagerly, I dropped my summer-activities money into the offering plate the following Sunday. But to my dismay, that cash never came back around.

What gives, God? I wondered.

I give to you, and you give it back. Isn't that how this deal works?

Unfortunately, much of our lives and our faith can be built on invisible half-truths. Hunting down these half-truths is difficult, not only because they are elusive but also because we don't necessarily want them to be found! We are comfortable with our own vision of the good life, whatever it entails and however inaccurate it might be. As a result, believing that the life *we* aspire to is where joy is truly found, we avoid contemplating what God had in store for us all along.

It's a costly diversion, mostly because by thinking we were meant only for the "good life" of our own construction, we start viewing suffering as the opposite of all that we deserve.

At first blush, this line of thinking is quite natural: Who wants career aspirations that forever go unmet? Who longs for challenging health issues? Who hopes for strained relationships?

Nobody—that's who.

So how is it that all those "bad" things and more could possibly be part of God's plan?

Suffering, whether self-inflicted or not, can be debilitating. Even Scripture says we should "rejoice with those who rejoice; mourn with those who mourn" (Romans 12:15). If we rejoice at times and mourn at others, then wouldn't it stand to reason that suffering and joy are magnetically opposed?

But what if we have it all wrong?

What if God intends for us to experience suffering *so that* we can know true joy? Jesus said in John 16:33, "I have told you these things [regarding the coming of the Holy Spirit after his return to heaven], so that in me you may have peace. In this world you will have trouble. But take heart! I have overcome the world."

Note that he didn't say, *if* you have trouble. No, he was saying that in this life, things will not always go our way, and that reality is *part of God's plan*. But that's not all he said, because on the heels of that somewhat grim reality check, he said we should "take heart."

Rather than seeing the troubles of this world as either a result of our own failures (which they sometimes are) or God's punishment toward the world for sin (which it might be), we can see every challenge in our lives as a thorn in our flesh that God has intentionally ordained to be used to glorify him.

Did God Really Say . . .?

In the garden of Eden, before sin entered the world, Satan's great plan was to tempt Eve to believe that God was withholding the good life from Adam and her. If they truly wanted to experience life to the fullest, the Enemy's thinking went, then Adam and Eve should eat from the Tree of Knowledge of Good and Evil. The implications here were that the couple's life could be *better than it was* and that *obedience to God* was blocking their ability to live as they deserved. In taking and eating the forbidden fruit, Adam and Eve acted on the doubts they had regarding God's plan for them, and they reached for the control they believed was theirs. In doing so, they ushered in the evil that still ravishes our world today.

It's important to notice that the serpent of Genesis 3, whom we learn in Revelation 12:9 is Satan, is there in the garden of Eden making *true statements*. But that doesn't mean he was being truthful. Interesting, don't you think? What Satan did was take truth and twist it a little, to fracture the foundation of trust that existed between humans and God.

"You will not certainly die" (Genesis 3:4) was a true statement, in a sense. The fruit wasn't poisoned, and those who partook would not immediately, physically die. "Your eyes will be opened" was also a true statement (v. 5). But rather than having their eyes opened by receiving desirable knowledge or enlightenment, Adam and Eve felt the curtain of their innocence being ripped in two.

And then there was this one: "You will be like God" (Genesis 3:5). This was not just a play on the couple's pride; rather, it was the distortion of a good desire (believing in our identity as image bearers of God) into something that is evil to its core (insisting that we humans be God instead).

In other words, once Adam and Eve started believing these half-truths, their view of God was dramatically altered, giving way to their committing sin. But the seed of doubt had been planted several verses earlier when the serpent began talking to Adam and Eve.

In reading Genesis 2, we see that God purposefully identifies himself in the special creation story of Adam and Eve, the story where he instructs them not to eat of the tree in the garden. Time and again, he is called the Lord God. The word "God" in Hebrew is translated from the name *Elohim*, which drives at the heart of God's power, justice, and rule. This is the name of God we see in Genesis 1 as he created the heavens and the earth. But in Genesis 2 he added to his name the word "Lord," or in Hebrew, *Yahweh.* This word is synonymous with the God of the covenant people. This is not just any god or false deity from antiquity; this is the God of Israel, the God who later would make a covenant with Abraham and deliver Israel from Egypt.

Do you see what is happening here? The serpent set the trajectory for where he wanted to take Adam and Even when he first spoke, saying, "Did God really say . . . ?" while conveniently omitting the half of God's name that assured Adam and Eve of God's loving-kindness toward them and isolating the name of God that could be misconstrued such that God was powerful but not personal. The real genius of the attack was deconstructing the nature of God as Adam and Eve saw it. A. W. Tozer once said, "What comes into your mind when you think about God is the most important thing about you."[2] Truly, every sin begins with our questioning whom we believe God is.

Rather than bringing sin into the world, Adam and Eve could have responded to the serpent's silent accusation with, "Your understanding is incomplete because that's not *all* of whom God is. He is not only mighty and just; he is also compassionate and loving. We will not eat from the tree, not because we think that an overbearing, power-hungry God has given us arbitrary rules to follow but because the Lord God who loves us says it is not in our best interest. He has proven his love for us in the way that he has provided for us, and we will demonstrate our love for him by obeying his commands. Though we do not understand fully, we trust him and *will not eat*."

Providence

I long to have that kind of response to Satan whenever he comes looking to trip me up. To trust God fully and act on that trust reflexively—that is a life well lived, I think. That is the life I want to lead.

Let's keep going.

At the heart of this trusting response is the doctrine of providence. Providence is the understanding that God is sovereign over creation not only in that he is powerful to control anything he chooses but also that he is actively guiding, influencing, and directing everything in the universe. Pastor John Piper defines providence as it relates to God as "the act of purposefully providing for, or sustaining and governing, the world."[3]

From Scripture, we see that the aim of all that God does is to glorify himself. God does all things for the sake of his own name (Isaiah 48:9–11). Piper continues: "'For his glory' does not mean to *get* glory which he doesn't already have but rather to display and vindicate and communicate his glory for the everlasting enjoyment of his people—that is, for all those who, instead of resenting God's self-exaltation, receive him as their supreme treasure."[4]

This is why God seeking his own glory is a good and moral thing. C. S. Lewis admitted that at one point he was repulsed by God's desiring praise from people because it sounded to him like a vain person seeking compliments. But he conceded that he misunderstood the reason God's glory is so central is because it is wrapped up in people experiencing his loving presence. "I did not see that it is in the process of being worshipped that God communicates His presence to men."[5] This sort of praise or celebration of God's glory is not foreign to the human experience. Lewis noted that as he began to reflect, it became obvious that everyone not only worships but desires to attribute praise to things they enjoy:

> The Psalmists in telling everyone to praise God are doing what all men do when they speak of what they care about. My whole, more general, difficulty about the praise of God depended on my absurdly denying to us, as regards the supremely Valuable, what we delight to do, what indeed we can't help doing, about everything else we value.[6]

The reason worshipping God is vastly different from our attempts to exalt ourselves is because we are not "ultimate." Lewis recognized that calling for compliments is a feeble attempt to make ourselves something we are not. And even if we are successful at self-glorification, the exchange of human-to-human praise satisfies neither the true longing of our hearts nor the heart-longing of those who laud us.

In other words, I can tell you how great you are, and that compliment might boost you in the moment. But it can't sustain you until the end. We're sustained only by magnifying God's greatness and by finding our identity in him.

WE'RE SUSTAINED ONLY BY MAGNIFYING GOD'S GREATNESS AND BY FINDING OUR IDENTITY IN HIM.

As Lauren mentioned, part of our story involves our daughter Zion being diagnosed with cancer when she was just a baby—twenty months old. If you've ever walked through cancer yourself or with a loved one, then you know how often cancer patients have to have IVs inserted into their veins so that medications, chemotherapy, and anesthesia can be delivered. This was certainly the case for Zion, and she *hated* needles. Every time a nurse had to "poke" our baby to establish an IV, Zion would wail as if the world were coming to an end. In her mind, it probably was.

On one occasion, a surgeon had to remove a diseased portion of her liver. You tell me: Are such actions considered harmful to Zion? So much poking and prodding and cutting! How could these things not be seen as harmful? Doctors vow to do no harm. This sure looked like harm to me!

The answer, of course, is that the purpose of the painful medical interventions was ultimately to make Zion's future better as the doctor removed the tumor that would eventually destroy our daughter if left to grow.

There's a lesson here for us too. This side of heaven, God's plan for us *must* include pain—in part because pain and suffering are the consequences of sin, in part because painful circumstances are a constant reminder that God is at work in our lives, redeeming even the most difficult parts of our earthly reality for his glory and for our good. Suffering in life, then, is surgery on our soul. It is the carving out of anything and everything that distracts us from magnifying God.

God not only allows pain to come into our experience but also *decrees* hard times for our lives. We get a peek into his motivation in Romans 8:28: "And we know that in all things God works for the good of those who love him, who have been called according to his purpose." This is the great promise that unlocks the doctrine of providence as not just good for God but good for us. This is not a promise that God works all things for our *temporal* pleasure, which is why that vacation money was not "ordained" to come back to me. No, this is a promise that the most evil and devastating events in our lives are part of a master plan we cannot see, a plan in which God is orchestrating all things for his eternal glory and our eternal joy.

SUFFERING IN LIFE, THEN, IS SURGERY ON OUR SOUL.

In John 9, Jesus passed by a man blind from birth, a man known in the area as the blind guy who sits and begs—a disgraceful identity, to be sure. In attempting to understand why this man suffered as he did, Jesus' disciples asked Jesus, "Rabbi, who sinned, this man or his parents, that he was born blind?" (v. 2). The disciples rightly understood that suffering is tied to sin, and so they asked whose sin it was that caused his suffering. The problem was, the blame belonged not to the man's parents but to relatives further up the line: Adam and Eve.

While the disciples attributed the blindness of the man outside the temple to the sin of the individual or his family, that wasn't the case at all. "Neither this man nor his parents sinned, but this happened so that the works of God might be displayed in him" (John 9:3). Why did this man suffer with blindness? For the sake of having God glorified through that pain.

Jesus would go on to heal this man, but the teaching dispensed before that healing is instructive to us all. Our struggles, handicaps, inabilities, and deficiencies are all given to us by God so that when he works through us in our weakness, it is obvious that God has shown himself strong.

In this way, pain is not the rival of joy but a requirement of it.

Suffering increases our capacity to rejoice.

It is only by walking through the archway of suffering that we set off down the road to the glade of gladness. This isn't a fake assurance that the job promotion you missed out on is preparing you for a bigger promotion than you would have had otherwise—let me be clear about that. It's just that if we are truly lovers of God, then we have recognized that *God being glorified* is a greater priority than our own comfort or pleasure, and thus any hardship that comes our way—while painful and often inexplicable—can still produce in us a greater joy.

By knowing Jesus intimately, in other words, we can rest assured that God is coordinating the worst of our temporal agony for the greatest of his eternal glory.

A CHANCE TO COLLECT YOUR THOUGHTS

At the end of each chapter, you'll find questions and journaling prompts that help you work through key concepts at your own pace and relative to the circumstances unfolding in your own life. You might log your responses in a notebook or on your phone; you might talk about one of the questions with a friend or family member over lunch; or you might simply sit with your thoughts before God for a few minutes, paying attention to how you're feeling as you read each question to yourself.

Take as much time as you need here before moving on in the book.

Falling Prey to a False Sense of What's Real

1. Describe a time when you unknowingly fell for a half-truth—or an outright lie. What were the circumstances? Once you realized what had happened, how did the experience make you feel?
2. What do you make of the fact that so many people are falling for the half-truth that if we make good decisions and do good things, God owes us a life that is "good"? Have you yourself ever fallen prey to this deception? If so, what factors caused you to believe it in the first place?
3. What thoughts or feelings surfaced for you as you read this chapter's assertion that "suffering in life . . . is surgery on our soul"? What assumptions about suffering does this idea challenge for you?

CHAPTER 2

EXPECTATIONS

The Alluring Illusion of Control

Eye the wisdom of God in all your afflictions.

—JOHN FLAVEL

MICHAEL

I don't remember the day I met Lauren Green, not because she's not memorable but because we both were somewhere around seven years old. Our families had just begun attending the same church, and there in Sunday school, learning Bible stories together, Lauren and I became familiar with each other. Then, throughout middle school and high school, we became friends—best friends, even. Which would have been great, except that as we entered our teenage years I didn't want to be best friends. Not *only* that, anyway.

Thankfully, after years of slowly building a foundation of friendship, I made the elusive transition from Lauren's friend to her boyfriend to, eventually, her fiancé. Finally, the summer after our junior year of college, I became her husband. Following our wedding I moved us into our first home, which was connected to a funeral home in a small town in south-central Oklahoma, an hour from where we both grew up. To the left was the only bar in town, and to the right was the funeral home with which we shared a driveway where the hearse came and went. Behind us was a chicken coop, and out our front door was a worm farm. You might say we were living the dream, if the dream were campy like that.

As our lives and careers developed, we moved back to Oklahoma City, where Lauren continued her work at the corporate office of her family's business, Hobby Lobby, and I began serving as a pastor on staff at Council Road Baptist Church, the same church where we'd met years prior and where both our families still attend. This was also when we felt the growing desire to investigate international adoption. We were four years into marriage and made just enough money to purchase our first house—a three-bedroom, two-bathroom starter home—and our lives were full of work and friends and happiness together. We anticipated that adding a baby to the mix would be a perfect next step.

Faith Versus Entitlement

Whether you are a planner who has your next five to ten years marked out by monthly goals or whether, like I do, you take things as they come, you have expectations for your life. Expectations are not inherently bad things, and life without any expectations at all quickly devolves into chaos. For example, we expect (and plan for) the seasons to arrive each year, spring after winter, summer after spring. We expect to be held accountable for following the laws of the land. We expect to ask for and offer a fair exchange of goods and payment in the marketplace. We expect people to do what they say they'll do. Expectations are part of the human experience.

For believers, though, we get ourselves into trouble when we become beholden to our expectations. When we identify unmet expectations, we typically are not pointing to sinful things we should repent of; rather, we are focused on our desire for good things, even godly things. But when we want God to give us good things more than we want God himself, we are guilty of idolatry. "Every man loves the mercies of God, but a saint loves the God of his mercies."[1]

But the great thrill of the Christian life is that when we see past our petitions to God, we behold God himself. And there we see the true treasure we wanted in material objects. There we see the true relationship that we thought we longed for in others. There we see the true approval we thought we desired in our success. "The best thing about Christ," Charles Haddon Spurgeon once wrote, is "Christ himself."[2]

WHEN WE IDENTIFY UNMET EXPECTATIONS, WE ARE FOCUSED ON OUR DESIRE FOR GOOD THINGS, EVEN GODLY THINGS.

God tells us in many ways exactly how he acts. Some of those acts are awe-inspiring, such as when we read in Psalm 147:8–9 that God "covers the sky with clouds; he supplies the earth with rain and makes grass grow on the hills. He provides food for the cattle and for the young ravens when they call."

Some are comforting, such as the promise given in Isaiah 41:10, which says, "So do not fear, for I am with you; do not be dismayed, for I am your God. I will strengthen you and help you; I will uphold you with my righteous right hand."

Others are terrifying, as is the case with the threat recorded in Psalm 52:4–5: "You love every harmful word, you deceitful tongue! Surely God will bring you down to everlasting ruin: He will snatch you up and pluck you from your tent; he will uproot you from the land of the living." But all are good: "The LORD is good to all; he has compassion on all he has made" (Psalm 145:9).

What happens when we start placing expectations on how God will or should act based on our interpretation of Scripture and our unexamined assumptions of life itself? I call these "entitled expectations." Entitled expectations make assumptions regarding how life should go and regarding our ability to control God, other people, or even the laws of nature to bend the outcomes in our favor. An entitled expectation reveals itself whenever we are frantically grasping to hold things that we were never meant to control.

Our expectations expose myriad ways we believe we can be God for ourselves. For example, early in our friendship, I remember being *stunned* that despite my kind and intentional care for Lauren (if I do say so myself), she didn't reciprocate in any sort of romantic way. Later, I'd be *shocked* that Lauren and I weren't spared specific financial burdens, given that we were consistent givers to our local church. We'd both be *perplexed* as to why, after years of faithful full-time ministry work, God didn't see fit to have us get pregnant or to have any adoptions work out. I could go on, but every example would point to the same takeaway: the fact that we were so deeply disappointed when things didn't go our way exposed the fact that we held expectations for how God *absolutely* should act.

OUR EXPECTATIONS EXPOSE MYRIAD WAYS WE BELIEVE WE CAN BE GOD FOR OURSELVES.

Throughout those seasons Lauren and I would have told you that we believed in God, loved God, and longed to follow God with our whole hearts, but those truths weren't getting translated into our actions. And Jesus said we will be known by our actions, what he called in Luke 6:44 the "tree" being "recognized by its own fruit."

In all candor, our fruit had rotted.

Our fruit had started to stink.

The most famous sufferer in the Old Testament was a man named Job. He was a faithful man, so upright that God essentially made him a bull's-eye for Satan to throw darts at. In a fascinating exchange between God and Satan, God upheld Job as a righteous servant, prompting Satan to go after Job to prove that this man would not remain faithful if harm came his way.

In a flash, Job lost everything that mattered to him—his possessions, his children, his business, his livestock, and his health. We would forgive a man in this state for shaking his fist at the heavens and cursing God, but that's not what Job did. Rather than fall prey to the belief that he was entitled to the life God had originally blessed him with, Job recognized that all of life was a gift from God. "Naked I came from my mother's womb," Job said, "and naked I will depart. The LORD gave and the LORD has taken away; may the name of the LORD be praised" (Job 1:21).

To be sure, Job was a sinner—just like you and me. In his suffering, he asked real questions of God and felt real emotions about his plight, sinking so low at one point as to question why he'd ever been born (Job 3). He tolerated the friends in his life whose bad advice only made matters worse. But through it all, as Job 1:22 says, "In all this, Job did not sin by charging God with wrongdoing."

I've always loved that line from Job, spoken right in the midst of his suffering: "May the name of the LORD be praised." Such a bold declaration! And yet you get the sense from Job's long-standing faithfulness that he meant every syllable he spoke. A person can't say, "May the name of the Lord be praised" during the worst bout of suffering unless he or she has spent a *long time* praising the Lord.

Job had been praising the Lord.

Later in this chapter we'll look at the fact that Job did grieve his losses—the same way that you and I would. But he never caved to cursing God. He stayed faithful through it all.

Back to those friends of Job's: Consider Bildad, who encouraged Job to repent. "But if you will seek God earnestly and plead with the Almighty," he said, "if you are pure and upright, even now he will rouse himself on your behalf and restore you to your prosperous state" (Job 8:5–6). Notice the if-then idea: Bildad essentially said, "Hey, Job, if you will do your part, then God will do his."

We may not say it as bluntly today, but isn't this our expectation too? We expect that if we remain faithful—you know, "do our stuff"—then God will do stuff for us.

Here's the takeaway: If we are going to remain faithful, even as we're still quite flawed, we must find our footing in the doctrines of who God has revealed himself to be. By knowing Scripture, we can know more fully what we should expect out of this life here on earth as well as throughout eternity. When our expectations about life are shaped by God as Creator of all things, reality can then be informed by truth.

Let me demonstrate this idea with a story. In her current (immature, undeveloped, unsophisticated) stage of life, our daughter Zion sees Lauren and me as her providers—something of a Santa and Mrs. Claus. Here's how this plays out: If Zion clues us in on something she wants at a store, for example, we usually respond by telling her she can ask for the toy or gizmo for her birthday. We then confirm her greatest fear about what this means: "We are not buying it today," we say, which is when she fixes her gaze on one of us and says with all earnestness, "But I really, really, *really* want it, guys!"

The last time this happened, to up the ante on her pleading,

Zion led with, "Mommy, Daddy, I know how much you love me . . ."

Well played, right?

If you love me, you'll do what lovable me wants. This stuff gets in our hearts when we're *young.*

You can imagine Zion's disappointment that day when the stuffed animal she just *knew* she was getting stayed put on the shelf in our local Hobby Lobby.

When it comes to God, we can think that finding just the right words to say will get us the things we want. We may not beg God as ferociously as a child begs for a toy at the store, but we can conjure strategies that might bend his will toward ours. We can easily fall into a trap where we look longingly for things we do not have and wonder why God has not blessed us with what he has given to others. It could be a better job, improved health, stronger relationships, greater notoriety, esteemed respect, or material possessions. None of these things are bad; they are all good gifts from God.

This common argument sees life as a game in which you must master the rules to move through the board to victory. That is not how God has created our lives to work, and Job eventually realized the false understanding Bildad had about life and success.

Gifts Are Not Givens

As I write this, I am on an airplane wrestling with these concepts. I search desperately for some quasi-productive way to distract myself from the writing deadline that looms. As I do, I stumble upon a writing-prompt video focused on the word "abundance." The instructor says that to realize greater abundance in my life I should develop a mantra such as, "I am free from worry." Or "I am surrounded by love." Or "Money flows easily to me." This alluring false teaching causes us to believe that we can name and claim our success through an incantation. This is not only futile; it's destructive. The reason entitled expectations are so poisonous is not because they do or do not come to pass but because of the way they affect our hearts.

This plays on the life we had in the garden before sin, building on a half-truth that humankind originally existed in Paradise. It even plays on the future for all those who are in Christ and will reign with him over the universe with God forever. Yet, while material prosperity was the reality God created us *in*, it was not the existence God created us *for*. That is to say, in the garden of Eden, Adam and Eve had every material thing they could ever want. Yet when they lost it all, they realized that what they really had wanted was God. They were created to enjoy the *presence of God*—and this alone.

The same is true for us.

When God created Adam and Eve, he gave them animals to rule over and plants to eat. He placed them in Paradise and gave them a special purpose. It is inherent to who we are: we, too, were made in God's image. In the ancient Near East, pagan religions would create idols in the image of the god they represented. By contrast, the creation account depicts God as creating humans to be his representatives. We are created to reflect him and to participate in ruling his creation—but not in whatever way we see fit. We are *his* image, not our own, which means that we are to participate in creation in a manner that aligns with how God himself would care for creation. And in seeing ourselves as stewards of all creation rather than owners, we humbly work to be fruitful and multiply for his glory, not our own.

While this may sound scandalous to you, you and I were not "created for abundance," as common Christian thinking goes these days; we were created for worship. Yes, Jesus told us he has come to give us "life, and have it to the full" (John 10:10), but this abundant life comes only as we follow the injunction of Matthew 6:33, which says, "But seek first his kingdom and his righteousness, and all these things will be given to you as well." The abundant life Jesus spoke of is eternal, not temporal. Temporary abundance may come to you in life—in love, family, marriage, business, finances, career, opportunity, or fame. But if it does come, it is a gift, not a given. It isn't the ultimate abundance we're assured.

WHEN WE TREAT GIFTS FROM GOD AS GIVENS, WE DENY GOD THE VERY WORSHIP HE CREATED US TO GIVE TO HIM.

And that gets to the heart of why expectations can become so dangerous. When we treat gifts from God as givens, we deny God the very worship he created us to give to him. This is at the core of why entitled expectations are damning: They stifle the God-glorifying praise that our souls were fashioned to express at every moment of the day. They force us to demand things of God that he never promised we would have.

"And he is not served by human hands, as if he needed anything. Rather, he himself gives everyone life and breath and everything else" (Acts 17:25). At this very moment, "he [Jesus] is before all things, and in him all things hold together" (Colossians 1:17). The Holy Spirit intercedes continually for us (Romans 8:26), which means that the Holy Trinity is involved in every moment of your day and mine. There is not a single moment during which God Almighty is not actively present and providing for our every need. No one has ever inhaled a mundane puff of oxygen. Every life-sustaining breath is a divine gift from the Creator. There has never been a coincidental sunny day that lifted you from despair. There will never be a surprise encounter at the coffee shop with someone who said just the thing you needed to hear. Along these lines, every natural disaster, car accident, cancer diagnosis, and difficult conversation between spouses is also from God.

Everything we have is a gift from God. John the Baptist knew this well. When his disciples came to him, concerned that the crowds that once followed John were now turning to follow Jesus, they were protesting that these were John's crowds that his ministry had worked hard to serve and grow. "To this John replied, 'A person can receive only what is given them from heaven'" (John 3:27). Everything we have is a gift. "Every good and perfect gift is from above, coming down from the Father of the heavenly lights, who does not change like shifting shadows" (James 1:17).

James 4 teaches us that we should not expect anything, instead recognizing that all is dependent on God: "Now listen, you who say, 'Today or tomorrow we will go to this or that city, spend a year there, carry on business and make money.' Why, you do not even know what will happen tomorrow. What is your life? You are a mist that appears for a little while and then vanishes" (vv. 13–14). This reminder from James that we are God's creation and that he is the eternal Creator helps us to reorder our expectations accordingly.

James continued: "Instead, you ought to say, 'If it is the Lord's will, we will live and do this or that.' As it is, you boast in your arrogant schemes. All such boasting is evil" (vv. 15–16). James rebuked the expectation itself as evil because by declaring that we know the future, we are saying we are equal to God. This isn't meant to make us legalistic in the way that we talk about business plans but rather to prompt us continually to remind ourselves that it is God who ultimately determines whether our business, our relationships, and our plans succeed or fail. A right view of God's sovereignty allows us to give him praise in both the prosperous providences and the painful providences alike.

If we were created to reflect the glory of God to the world, then anytime we miss recognizing God for his work, we are robbing him of the praise he created us to give him. We have not been appointed stewards over the abundance of provision that exists in this world so we can waste our lives finding pleasure in experiencing what God has created. Rather, all creation has been placed under our care so that we may find pleasure in experiencing God himself. Creation is meant to point us to the Creator and drive us to worship him.

ANYTIME WE MISS RECOGNIZING GOD FOR HIS WORK, WE ARE ROBBING HIM OF THE PRAISE HE CREATED US TO GIVE HIM.

What might this look like? For starters, the next time you share a meal with people you love, pause to thank God for his provision. Truly reflect on the reality that you are going to enjoy food that someone else worked to help provide for you. The salad you will eat was dependent on God providing the proper weather conditions so the various ingredients could grow. It was dependent on a farmer, who planted and harvested. Some manner of cleaning or inspection took place. The food was packaged by someone else and shipped by another. A grocer stocked the shelves with the produce, and when you bought it, a cashier assisted in processing the payment. Every step along the path, the providence of God was bringing you the food you are about to enjoy. Just about every step depended on someone else working to make that meal.

Something powerful happens when we give God praise for specific ways he has worked in our lives, especially in ways that are easily overlooked. John Flavel wrote, "Be exact in discharging the duties of those relations which so gracious a Providence has led you into. Do not abuse the effects of so much mercy and love to you. The Lord expects praise wherever you have comfort."[3]

Empty Rooms

When Lauren and I first started the adoption process, we were young and optimistic and felt excited to start our family in this way. In the international adoption process, each country has its own stipulations that govern who can qualify to adopt from their country, but every country we were interested in adopting from required that adoptive parents be at least twenty-five years of age. So on my twenty-fifth birthday, Lauren enthusiastically offered up the idea that she thought it was time to start the process. After conversation and prayer, I agreed, and we started working on the application the next day.

Flash-forward five years and we were still childless. After pursuing adoption for three years in Uganda, leaders in that country decided to close the program. We considered the options, and switched to another program, and began down that path, only for that program to be halted as well. What had started as an exciting journey had deteriorated into a confusing and exhausting process. It was then that I began to wonder if perhaps we were not destined to begin our family through adoption. Maybe we should try to get pregnant instead.

With renewed hope for growing our family, we headed full-force down that path in our late twenties, but after months with no "guess what!" announcements to offer friends or family, we started looking to doctors for clarity on whether this was a random situation or if a deeper issue was lurking somewhere. At the end of all the testing, it became clear that having biological children was going to be a real challenge for us. Of course, our first reaction was to ask what we could do to increase our chances for having a child. We wanted the doctors to lay out the plan to fix the issue, as if the problem were irritated tonsils or a bum knee. The fact was, there was no easy answer or magic formula available. There were suggestions. But after pursuing various options, we found ourselves right back where we'd started: childless, frustrated, sad.

So far, everything in life had gone according to our plan. The natural progression through school, getting married, starting a career—all of it had unfolded with ease. There was nothing we could not accomplish with a dose of determination and a dash of positive attitude. Yet here was a mountain we were powerless to climb. Here stood a struggle in which all our strength benefited us little, and all our effort seemed impotent at best.

That little starter home we bought, with hopes of filling it to overflowing with children? Well, five years later, we moved out. While there was some real excitement for our second home that was right across the street from some close friends, leaving that first house only magnified the emptiness we felt. The spare rooms that waited all those years to be transformed from an office or a guest bedroom into nurseries echoed the dull pain of the one way our lives had not changed since moving into that place.

In five long years, we had not brought home a single child, and each passing month became just another way to mark our childless time.

We continued to pursue every medical intervention that made sense for us. But our expectations shifted. It was natural for us to expect our bodies to function in a way that is normal, but when our plans didn't pan out, our oblivious optimism devolved into anxiety. What would this mean for us? For our future? For our lives as lovers of God?

A CHANCE TO COLLECT YOUR THOUGHTS

Sit with your thoughts before God for a few minutes, paying attention to how you're feeling as you read each question to yourself. Take as much time as you need before moving on in the book.

Our Expectations of Good and Godly Things

1. How well do you relate to the temptation of wanting the good things God can give you more than you want God himself? What is one practice that helps you long for God more than for what God can do for you? What would you hope to gain by elevating this practice this week?
2. Why do you think it's so hard for Jesus' followers not only to believe the truth about him but also to demonstrate those beliefs in our actions day after day?
3. What thoughts or feelings rise to the surface for you as you consider the assertion that "everything you have is a gift from God"? In what ways do you naturally embrace that reality? In what ways do you resist?

CHAPTER 3

ANXIETY

When Worries Come Our Way

Do not be anxious about anything, but in every situation, by prayer and petition, with thanksgiving, present your requests to God.

—THE APOSTLE PAUL

LAUREN

When Michael and I first learned that Zion had a tumor on her liver, we had no idea what we would do or where that input would lead. The initial shock to our systems was intensely disruptive, and I remember feeling deeply grateful for the flood of calls and texts that came in. Family members, neighbors, and friends from every corner of the world reached out to remind us that they were praying for us, that they loved us, that things would be okay. Those touchpoints were all important, but to this day one stands out above the rest as ministering most meaningfully to my mind and heart.

Doug, a longtime pastor friend who served in Lexington, Oklahoma, the crosstown rival of the small town where Michael and I lived as newlyweds, Purcell, gave us a call that was not only pastoral but also prophetic. "The period you are in now is the worst part," Doug said, "because so much is unknown. Once you know what you are up against, things will become easier." I wasn't at all sure that anything would ever feel easy again, but the "worst part" thing I could sure relate to. Life during that week felt like a nightmare we'd never wake up from.

Zion's tumor had been caught in a routine medical exam, prompting our pediatrician to tell us to head to the Oklahoma Children's Hospital emergency room right away. Shocked and confused, we drove straight there and watched slack-jawed as nurses admitted our baby to a tenth-floor room in the cancer wing.

Twenty-four hours before, Michael and I were having a relaxed lunch with Zion and several of our family members. Now, we were crammed into a hospital room with a bevy of nurses and a team of doctors talking with us about procedures, statistics, and treatments. As if on cue, those nurses all eyed one of the doctors as he passed us a stack of release papers requesting our permission for Zion's test results to be shared with the medical community for research.

The doctor began to explain the mass they'd found on Zion's liver, saying that while he would need to perform a biopsy before he had conclusive information, he believed that Zion could, in fact, have cancer. I remember telling myself that this couldn't be happening, that somehow we had taken a wrong turn and ended up in someone else's life.

Michael and I had just been wrapping up the remainder of our parental leaves and slowly transitioning back into our normal work routines when we ended up in the hospital with Zion that day, with fear of outright tragedy gripping our hearts.

Mere hours before we'd known about the tumor, Michael had buckled our giddy, carefree daughter into her car seat so that she'd be safe en route to her doctor's appointment. Now, the realization sank in me with a thud that we hadn't been able to keep her safe at all. This diagnosis was troubling, inescapable, and real. Cancer had paved our path. Everything relating to Zion's uncertain diagnosis felt totally beyond our control.

Misplaced Hope in Control

When Michael and I were talking about the frustrating idea that control is nothing more than an illusion, he reminded me of a trip his family took to Branson, Missouri, when he was ten years old. There he'd gone to his first magic show, and as is the case with most kids when they first take in magic tricks, he'd been enthralled. Throughout the act the magician made a woman levitate, caused a random audience member to disappear, and literally conjured a helicopter from thin air. The show was so electric that Michael decided then and there that somehow he, too, would become a magician.

Between you and me, I'm glad that career path didn't pan out.

Anyway, Michael said that right after the show, his parents agreed to buy him a magician's starter kit, complete with a wand, a loaded card deck, a fake coin, and a host of other aspiring-magician goodies. For the rest of that trip, he spent hours practicing, hoping to master the magician craft so that he could become the best of the best. But as he made his way through the kit's instruction manual, Michael realized what you and I and most savvy people know, which is that magic isn't magic at all; it's misdirection and nothing more. It isn't some special power that makes a helicopter appear onstage; smoke and mirrors are all you need.

Magic tricks are nothing more than well-orchestrated distractions that cause your mind to buy a lie. The woman wasn't floating; she was being upheld by invisible wires. The audience member didn't disappear; he probably scurried offstage to hide behind the black curtain we hadn't noticed before. The helicopter didn't appear out of thin air—come to think of it, maybe it did. Michael didn't have an explanation for that.

The Illusion of Control

If I were to name the most significant era in contemporary history in terms of ushering in generation after generation of what I empathetically refer to as "control freaks," it would have to be the

Enlightenment. During the seventeenth and eighteenth centuries, this intellectual movement swept through Europe, introducing a whole new worldview to unsuspecting people and teaching them what to think about God, humanity, nature, and reason itself. You could think of this period as the time when people started *knowing stuff for sure*. During the Enlightenment, scholars believed they finally understood the universe in its entirety. They finally understood the goal of existence. They finally understood how to be happy. They finally understood how to be free. For once, they had control of their lives, not realizing control was not theirs to have.

Marching through the centuries to come, technological advancements only cemented this illusion of control, causing our forebears to mistakenly believe that they, too, had far more control over life and its myriad outcomes than could ever actually be gained. But despite our ability to communicate instantaneously with anyone anywhere around the globe, order the latest best-seller with same-day delivery, and adjust our bank accounts or book airline tickets from the palm of our hand, eventually we find ourselves standing in a hospital room, our daughter lying helplessly in a steel-frame bed, the realization slowly sinking in that we don't control much at all. And that's when anxiety sets in.

Psychologist Dr. John Townsend is a family friend, and recently he explained to me that the negative emotion often most closely associated with the concept of control, or a lack of it, is anxiety. The control/anxiety correlation rang true. The growing illusion that we have more control of our lives than previous generations seems to be leading us to a place of greater anxiety, not less. True, some types of fear, worry, and anxiety are normal and healthy. For instance, if I'm preparing for a talk I'm going to give to a room full of people, I might feel dread because I haven't had time to carefully craft my words. I might experience a loss of appetite over the fact that I keep overcommitting myself. I might be worried that I'll embarrass myself by getting tripped up in my words. But these are what I would call situational fears and anxieties, which can be *productive* in the end. These concerns can serve to make me rehearse well between now and the day of my talk, to pray with a little greater intention, and to fine-tune my focus once I'm standing there onstage. Far more concerning are the fears and anxieties that *don't* rise and fall with circumstances but rather just keep rising year after year.

In her marvelous book *The Cost of Control*, author Sharon Hodde Miller explores the connection between our desire for control and anxiety disorders. She wrote that "study after study has shown a link between feeling out of control and experiencing anxiety disorders."[1] Additionally, Miller noted that anxiety in general has shown to have increased among the American public, with the most significant increase in anxiety being among young people.[2] In a study of college students, the survey taken between 2011 and 2018 found that "rates of moderate to severe anxiety rose from 17.9 percent in 2013 to 34.4 percent in 2018."[3] That's one in three students being hamstrung in their ability to live their daily lives with any sort of normalcy at all, and postpandemic the numbers are likely even higher than that. This research seems to show that on some level, there is now a simmering fear that we might actually lose the control we think we've gained. It is this fear that has led to greater worry and anxiety in our lives. The goal is to consider how we might, with God's help, fight against unnecessary feelings of anxiety and worry.

The Reality of Control

Jesus provided clear thoughts on fear and anxiety in the middle of the best-known message he ever delivered during his earthly ministry, the Sermon on the Mount: "Therefore I tell you, do not worry about your life, what you will eat or drink; or about your body, what you will wear. Is not life more than food, and the body more than clothes?" (Matthew 6:25). This advice is nothing new; for example, even the Buddha encouraged people not to be anxious and to free themselves from the cares of this world so that they might achieve nirvana. But what makes Jesus' claim here particularly interesting is how he grounded this exhortation in truth.

Jesus gave two analogies to consider, both offered ironically, I think. First, he said to consider the birds of the air and how they always, always have food to eat, despite their never harvesting or producing a crop. Birds don't have fields or barns, Jesus was insinuating, so how do they get their food? That's right: God provides it. God will provide for us too.

Second, Jesus said to consider the flowers of the field, whose petals are likened to clothes. A flower with no petals would look like a disgraced weed, but how are flowers supposed to find clothes? That's right: God provides them. God will provide for us too.

What does all this mean? It's this: The weapon to fight worry isn't just in thinking, *Because things work out for birds and flowers, I should be fine, right?* Rather, the reason we should not worry is because God is sovereign over everything that happens to us. And not only is God in control, but he *cares* for you and me. Remember that Jesus closed this little monologue by asking, "Are you not much more valuable than they?" (Matthew 6:26).

So, what can relieve our anxiety? The power of God and the scope of his sovereignty matched with the love of God and the depth of his devotion. God's power combined with God's love—*that's* what puts us at ease.

GOD'S POWER COMBINED WITH GOD'S LOVE—*THAT'S* WHAT PUTS US AT EASE.

No matter how dark things seem, no matter how long the suffering runs, you are not alone in your peril, because God is near. You don't need to fear. You don't need to be anxious. He's near. He sees. And he cares.

A Truth to Guide Our Steps

Now, I'm not trying to pile on here, but I need to remind you and me both that overestimating the control we think we possess is not only mistaken but sinful. Our late friend Timothy Keller said it this way: "It takes pride to be anxious. I am not wise enough to know how my life should go."[4] In other words, overestimated control finds its root in our pride.

Keller also reminded us that "worry is not believing God will get it right, and bitterness is believing God got it wrong."[5] Yikes. That one hits a little too close to home.

The reason we should not be anxious is because at its core, anxiety is a lack of trust in God. Anxiety reveals areas of our lives where we find ourselves questioning the goodness or the power of God. If God were truly good and all-powerful, the thinking goes, then I wouldn't find myself in a hospital with my daughter fighting cancer. Anxiety grips my heart because I don't have the power to do *anything* to change the situation I'm in.

The apostle Peter exhorted believers to "cast all your anxiety on him because he cares for you" (1 Peter 5:7). The care of the Father is the compelling reason that we should cast our anxiety

> OUR FATHER *CARES* FOR US. HE LONGS TO RECEIVE OUR CARES.

on God. Now, if you are thinking that this is easier said than done, I'm with you. The fact is, there are real physiological factors that can cause ongoing anxiety to be an issue for people, and no amount of reciting 1 Peter 5:7 is going to help. Sometimes, clinical attention is needed, which is why therapeutic professionals exist.

Still, for all anxiety, regardless of its cause or its severity, we are benefited by remembering that God is not indifferent toward us. We aren't an inconvenience to him. No, no, our Father *cares* for us. He longs to receive our cares. "We cannot present a reason for Christ to finally close off his heart to his own sheep," author Dane Ortlund reminds us. "No such reason exists."[6]

Casting Our Cares

Although it wasn't the answer that Michael and I had hoped for, our friend Doug had been right. "The period you are in now is the worst part," he had said as we tried to make sense of Zion's cancer diagnosis and all that lay ahead for us. "Once you know what you're up against, things will become easier for you."

How true that proved to be. Once Michael and I had a plan of action for Zion, we could focus all our attention on praying for the next step to go well. We recruited friends, family members, and strangers alike to join us in that effort, learning at some point in the process that a radio station all the way down in Australia had heard about our story and was asking their listeners to pray.

Six days following the initial diagnosis, Zion was being admitted to the hospital for surgery for the tumor on her liver to be removed. We felt anxious—of course we did. She was so little—and so new to us. But God knew what he was doing. We felt sure of that as well.

To our surprise, as we made our way down the hospital corridor in search of Zion's room, the first nurse we caught sight of turned toward us, looked at our little girl, and said, "Oh my goodness! Is this Zion? I prayed for her this morning!"

Several hours prior, the nurse had learned of our story from Twitter. Our friend Lee Strobel had posted about us, but this nurse had no clue that we lived in Oklahoma City, let alone that Zion would be her patient that same day. It was one in a whole host of reminders that day that the same God who fed every bird and clothed every flower would provide for our family that day. We could cast our cares on him . . . and boy, did we have many to cast. But it was okay. His Word had said so. We could cast every last care at the feet of our Father because our Father cared deeply for us.

Because He Lives

Doug had been able to speak into our lives so effectively in our moment of crisis because he'd faced real crises of his own. Doug and his wife had walked the path of childhood cancer with their firstborn who would defy the odds and was a delightful middle schooler who loved church, his friends, and the Cubs.

But despite those beautiful bonus years, cancer would return and take their son's life.

Nearly two thousand people came to the memorial service, roughly the population of Lexington itself, many of whom were dressed in Cubs gear. This had been the young man's singular request, and everyone who could, complied.

A memory of sitting in the balcony at that service came to mind as I held Zion the same week that she received her diagnosis. It was the memory of watching our friends crying on the front row as the congregation sang the chorus of "Because He Lives." God really does hold the future, you know. And because of this reality, we no longer need to hold fast to fear.

A CHANCE TO COLLECT YOUR THOUGHTS

Sit with your thoughts before God for a few minutes, paying attention to how you're feeling as you read each question to yourself. Take as much time as you need before moving on in the book.

Seeing Truth in Our Blinding Circumstances

1. When have you experienced a "shock to the system" like the one described upon receiving Zion's cancer diagnosis? What was that like for you? What emotions prevailed at that time?
2. The beginning of our journey through Zion's cancer ordeal was described as "troubling, inescapable, and real." Do these words resonate with your experience too? What other adjectives might you use?
3. What has your experience with anxiety been like during difficult seasons in your life? Have you ever associated anxiety with the need to control? Do you think such a connection exists?
4. What do you make of the idea that God promises to provide for us, even in highly practical ways—the food we eat, the clothes we wear, the basic needs we share? When have you experienced what you'd consider "divine provision"? What made the provision divine?

CHAPTER 4

GRIEF

How Loss Feels and How to Respond

Our sense of power in this world may be largely delusional, but nonetheless we grieve when we lose it.

—DIANE LANGBERG

LAUREN

It was a crisp fall afternoon, and from my office window I could see that the grass was already turning the familiar shade of Oklahoma's wintery sandy-brown. Zion's cancer had been in remission for ten months, and life seemed to be finding a new normal—or as normal as things could be for the year 2020.

I turned on my laptop and ran my hands across the familiar keys to enter my password, a function my fingers knew well. My computer ready to go, I geared up for a Zoom call with my team. I work at the Hobby Lobby corporate office as a ministry director, where I'm privileged to collaborate with leaders across the country that Hobby Lobby partners with on community engagement.

My team and I gather in person quarterly for an extended planning session, but due to pandemic restrictions, our meetings had transitioned to a digital platform. For our October 2020 meeting, we had a lot to cover, and I thought I was feeling the normal level of stress as we started the six-hour video call. After I offered an opening prayer, team members began to dive into their reports. Which is when I noticed something unusual: a certain tightness in my chest.

I had experienced this before, once on the anniversary of a painful marital conflict and once during a live interview about a controversial topic. I assumed the pain had been triggered by stress this time, too, given the long and important meeting ahead of me. Surely in a few minutes it would fade.

An hour later, it hadn't faded at all. If anything, it had worsened, and now I was annoyed. I texted one of my teammates a heads-up that I had to step away for a minute and needed him to cover for me, and I took a walk and breathed deeply, willing the tightening to loosen its grip. Several minutes later, I rejoined the call and faked being all right, even as three hours later I was still in pain and increasingly very afraid.

Six hours into my ordeal, I wrapped up the call, packed up my things, left the office, and drove myself to the emergency room. Tests were run and opinions were proffered: it had been a panic attack, nothing more.

As I left the hospital, it was already dark outside, and in the silence of the drive I tried to discern what all that had been about. Nothing came to mind, even as two days later, during a phone call with a psychologist friend, I was reminded how extraordinarily tough the previous twelve months had been.

If you've walked through an out-of-control season, then you've also walked through grief. The two are tight companions, united by the unknown. That day at the hospital, the grief I'd neglected to deal with was now showing up as a panic attack. When we face painful circumstances, we've got to register that pain. Otherwise, it will run roughshod through our bodies and hearts, leaving destruction in its wake.

The Fear of Being Brought Low

On the phone with my friend that day, he knew I had recently experienced the deeply sobering fear of losing my child to cancer. Even typing those words three years later, tears pool in my eyes. I feel the intensity of that fear all over again, the total lack of control.

Michael and I had prayed for seven long years for a child, and bringing Zion home and settling her into our family represented the highest of highs for me. Then, in a matter of weeks, my daughter had been diagnosed with a life-threatening tumor that was cancerous and had to come out. I lived for months standing face-to-face with the fear of losing her, of losing this new version of us.

The prospect of saying goodbye forever to my precious girl was terrifying to me, but throughout those months Michael and I stayed in fight mode, determined to help our girl win. We were focused on providing every possible bit of support for Zion: making her comfortable, making memories during the breaks we had from hospital stays, spending time together while quarantined as she sat for chemotherapy treatments.

It was an agonizing season marked by awful, awful things: surgery to remove the tumor, surgery to insert a catheter line for chemotherapy, training for at-home care, countless home-health medical-supply deliveries, education on cancer research, several rounds of chemotherapy, quarantining due to the chemotherapy's impact on her immune system, missing holidays and family trips.

At last, after an intense few months, better news arrived: *remission.*

Once Zion's cancer was in remission, we were ready to have life feel normal again, so we returned to life as usual. We felt joy over the remission and deep gratitude in our hearts for every second we had together now. But one thing Michael and I didn't do was take the time to process what we had just experienced. We didn't take time to lament.

Simply put, lament is expressing grief. I hadn't taken time to sit with my pain and process it all. Instead, I adopted one of the million ways that we can ignore our pain: denying it, stuffing it, glossing over it, or suppressing it. For me, I subconsciously decided to avoid my grief altogether. It was a form of toxic positivity, where I wanted to think only about the optimistic end to Zion's cancer experience. Things had turned out well, hadn't they? Why not just focus on that and move on? And honestly, I felt like I didn't deserve to grieve. Our girl made it through, and I knew other children who never made it to the remission stage. So I celebrated the good news of remission and moved on.

By the fall of 2020, when Zion had been in remission for ten months, the stress of my high-pressure work meeting had triggered my body to let me know that it was tired. It couldn't hold on to the pain from our experience with Zion's cancer any longer. My body had been keeping track and had hit a breaking point from months of suppressed grief.

A Word on Embodiment

In his groundbreaking book *The Body Keeps the Score*, research psychiatrist Bessel van der Kolk wrote of the brain, mind, and body connection and how we respond to trauma. Based on his extensive research into the subject, he concluded that trauma has an impact on the mental, emotional, neurological, and physiological self. Trauma ends up rewiring the brain and can cause a trauma survivor to experience constant stress and lead to a whole slew of physical problems.[1]

Van der Kolk studied different experiences that trauma stems from, including severe vehicle accidents, war, life-threatening experiences, abuse, and neglect. From the trauma survivors he worked with, he discovered that even when a traumatic experience was not remembered, either because it happened when a person was too young to recall or because the person's brain had blocked the memory, the trauma still had its effect on the body. The body was keeping the score, even if the memory didn't.

Trauma experts, therapists, and social workers dealing with children coming out of challenging circumstances have reiterated this phenomenon by studying how infants and young children are affected by traumatic events. Even though an infant has no memory of a trauma, the rewired brain will have an impact in physical and emotional manifestations later in life.[2] Our bodies really do permanently absorb what is happening to us emotionally, physically, and spiritually.

Genesis 1 provides a unified understanding of our emotional, physical, and spiritual selves as the parts that make each of us who we are. Truly, every part is interconnected to the other. From the creation account, we can see that every created thing was made with physical substance. Humanity was created with bodies, to work and exercise dominion, long before the fall in the garden, when sin came into the world.

In our Western culture, we often see our bodies as something to be pushed, driven to perform. For a culture that can also be focused on appearance, often the only time we think about our own bodies is when we are comparing them to another in terms of beauty or attractiveness. For the young, healthy, able-bodied person, outside of what we think of our physical appearance, we may not ever think about the limitations our body has.

In school we are taught to push our body in sports or deprive it of sleep to study all night. As a young parent, we may be rolling around on the ground with our kids, bearing the weight of growing babies and toddlers and forgetting to nourish our own bodies with food and water in the midst of chasing little ones.

The functionality and service that our bodies provide to us

is an afterthought. As Kelly Kapic explained in his book *You're Only Human*, "Even when we run into our inevitable limits, we often hang on to the delusion that if we just work harder, squeeze tighter, if we become more efficient, we can eventually gain control." He goes on to say, "When I complain about getting older, my wife sometimes laughs and says to me, 'You have two options: either you are getting older, or you are dead.' Denying our finitude cripples us in ways we don't realize."[3] And ultimately, he argues, if we deny our finitude and limits, it distorts how we view God.

We can tend to treat our bodies like a car. I drive a 2003 Toyota that has more than 230,000 miles on it. I love that it is reliable and low maintenance. I hardly think about my car because most times it is faithful to run the way it should. I hop in and buckle up, and it gets me from point A to point B. But the second my car doesn't run the way it should, I am reminded that my car must be tended to, cared for, and made to run properly.

For the past two months I've driven my old, faithful car around with the maintenance light flashing at me the entire time. It has been a busy season, and I kept meaning to take it in, but despite my good intentions, I still haven't made it to the shop. The car has continued to run, so I have just kept driving it. This week on my commute home from work, that maintenance light on my dash was suddenly joined by the "check engine" light and two other lights that could signal impending doom for me.

I was then paying very close attention to my car. Any slight noise or strange smell, and I was worried about what was happening under the hood. I was tuned in to my car and thinking about its care. In the same way that I was paying close attention to my car as I (finally!) navigated my way to the shop, you and I must remember to stay tuned in to our bodies, lest they choke and sputter and fail. This is especially true when we are experiencing emotional hardship in life and facing circumstances beyond our control. If we don't deal with the emotional effects of our pain, it will affect us physically. And our physical well-being dramatically impacts our ability to live healthy and free. Ask the friend with an autoimmune disease or the family member with a dreadful health diagnosis, and they will tell you that this is so.

Our own embodiment is an essential part of who we are as humans. We are created with a mind, soul, and a body. Each part of us was created by God intentionally and is a part of what makes each of us who we are. And each part of us is inextricably connected to the other parts of who we are. We should see our whole self—spiritual, emotional, and physical—as created with a purpose and with inherent value because of who we are as God's image bearers.

WE SHOULD SEE OUR WHOLE SELF AS CREATED WITH A PURPOSE AND WITH INHERENT VALUE BECAUSE OF WHO WE ARE AS GOD'S IMAGE BEARERS.

With this theological framework, we can see how the science of trauma has revealed such interconnectedness for the impact on the whole person. We are not beings who can section out one part of ourselves or our experiences and keep it locked away so that it will not affect the other aspects of our lives. We may try, in an unhealthy way, to compartmentalize. But in the end, unresolved grief, sorrow, and trauma will always come back to affect our lives, much as they did that fall morning in 2020 when my body sent me straight to the emergency room. If we want to live life optimally, we have to do the hard work of processing life's pain points.

The Usefulness of Lament

The idea of lament may be an unfamiliar concept to you, but in Scripture it shows up frequently. Old Testament scholars consider two-thirds of the book of Psalms to be psalms of lament.[4] There is also a book of the Bible named Lamentations, which is a recorded memorial to the pain and confusion the Israelites felt following the destruction of their city and its fall to Babylon.

The point is that the Bible is no stranger to lament. Lament is the expression of grief and sorrow. Lament is the process by which a person can verbalize, express, or even moan about the pains that have brought grief into their life. Lament is a way to voice our confusion about God's character and promises. Lament provides sacred dignity to our suffering.[5] We can look to the psalmists, who spent a great deal of time reflecting on and expressing their grief, to be a model for us to remember the significance of the process of lament.

Jesus himself practiced lament. Days before his crucifixion, Jesus received word that his close friend Lazarus was very ill. Lazarus and his sisters, Mary and Martha, were apparently friends who were more like family to Jesus, yet when the sisters sent word about their brother's poor health, Jesus delayed in coming to see them. By the time he arrived, it was too late. Lazarus had died and Mary and Martha were in mourning.

Jesus, being God, already knew this. Jesus knew when he delayed coming that when he arrived, he would find Lazarus dead. Jesus knew that Martha would respond in anger and Mary in despair. Jesus taught that he *was* the resurrection and the life. Jesus knew that a few moments from now he would do the impossible and raise Lazarus from the dead. Yet to the surprise of those around him, Jesus responded with grief.

"Jesus wept," John 11:35 reports. Because his friends were in pain, he cried.

The Bible shows us many examples of expressed lament as well as a Creator and heavenly Father who is willing to hear us out during our honest expressions of pain. Lament can be a prayerful proof of the relationship we have with God. Because when we turn toward God, we welcome deeper intimacy with him.

There is no doubt that grief has a dramatic effect on our emotional, physical, and spiritual lives, a pervasiveness that ought to motivate us to process our grief as healthfully and thoroughly as possible. As I neglected to deal with my pain, I subjected my self—my whole self—to unnecessary suffering. That this suffering manifested itself in my life physically should have come as no surprise.

Unresolved grief might show up as chest pains, tightness in your throat, or a fear of suffocating, just as I've experienced on previous occasions when having a panic attack. It may show up as a sleep disturbance—you feel exhausted but can't get your body to fall asleep. I experienced this in my grief during the weeks after we said goodbye to our baby boy, Ezra—the son who, despite our thinking we'd keep him forever, was stripped from our arms a mere twelve months after he joined our family. It might show up as body pains, muscle tension, a racing heart, eating disorders, digestive issues, and other manifestations that connect with your body.[6] But one thing is sure: unresolved grief *definitely* will show up.

God created us with emotions. When we see Jesus and his life on earth as both fully God yet fully man, we can observe the feelings that Jesus felt. For example, Jesus expressed joy (Hebrews 12:2), sorrow (John 11:33–35), anger (Matthew 23:33), compassion (Matthew 9:20–22; John 8:1–11), empathy (John 4:1–11), and agony (Luke 22:42).

One of the most comforting things for enduring seasons of grief is knowing that we are not alone. We have a Father in heaven who understands us. We have a Father who cares. Because of Christ's life on earth, "we do not have a high priest who is unable to empathize with our weaknesses, but we have one who has been tempted in every way, just as we are—yet he did not sin" (Hebrews 4:15). Like us, God has *grieved.* Through his Son, Jesus, he has grieved. And because of this, we can feel more than confident in bringing our full emotional experience to him.

Consider Jesus' life specifically regarding how he experienced grief. Isaiah 53:3 says he was a "man of suffering, and familiar with pain." As we saw in the account involving Lazarus, Jesus was in such a state of deep grief that he didn't just cry, he *wept.*

If you've ever seen someone truly weep, then you know how intense it can be. Our Savior, Jesus, has been there. He understands *intensity.* Imagine Jesus in his full humanity, bent over, groaning with tears. And let the image compel you toward him, toward the one who truly understands.

We don't honor God by ignoring or stuffing our emotions. As we follow Jesus' example, we honor whom he created us to be. When we create space to express our sorrows both to God and to others in safe and loving relationships, we reflect the authenticity he possessed.

As we come to Jesus in authenticity, our level of intimacy with him is enriched. As we lay down the facade we've been hiding behind, we allow him to make us whole.

Walking Well Through Grief

Grieving various losses alongside my husband has been an eye-opening experience for me, mostly because I've seen firsthand that people really do deal with grief in different ways. I remember being struck by the rhythm of how Michael and I would flow in and out of our toughest moments, as though we existed in opposing states much of the time. Every time Michael was feeling the heaviest weight of grief, I was lighter in mood. And when I was most profoundly weighed down by the grief, Michael was strong once again. It was as if God were granting us a measure of just-in-time grace so that we might feel the strength to bear each other's burden at just the right moments.

Still, while it was true that our seesaw cadence always made the grieving process easier, frustrations did arise. Grief can make you prickly, and on more occasions than Michael and I want to admit, our emotional depletion would cause us to lash out in anger at each other—generally speaking, a rare reaction for us. Extra grace was certainly required.

In her book *Suffering and the Heart of God*, trauma therapist Dr. Diane Langberg provides theological and practical considerations for how to process our painful experiences, such as the suggestion that we move toward healing from our past pains with three things: talking, tears, and time.[7]

After the loss of our son, Michael and I needed permission to talk about our feelings with each other, to reflect on who Ezra was to us, to try to find a way to honor his memory, and to express how we felt now that he was gone from our lives. Speaking truth about circumstances is always more honoring than speaking falsehood or ignoring reality altogether. The story matters, and the truth matters. Ezra mattered to us.

We also needed space to cry, to find an avenue for releasing our sadness and pain. The tears often came at unexpected, even inopportune, moments, times when grief snuck up on us like a thief. We've done our best to welcome them in, whenever and whyever they've come. During certain weeks and months, I've mused that God has really had his work cut out for him, given that according to Psalm 56:8 he is said to account for each of our tears. "Record my misery," the psalmist wrote. "List my tears on your scroll—are they not in your record?"

What kindness our Father extends to us, to see and capture our tears.

And finally, grieving has definitely taken its time. It takes time to adjust to the new normal that loss always leaves behind. I once read that it can take two to four years to "resolve" grief, and I audibly gasped. In my classic style, I'd pushed ahead, believing I could check grief off my list. When I realized it was not as easy as blowing through a three-step plan and moving on with life, I was the poster child for defeat. Now one year into saying goodbye to Ezra, I can see that the estimate was right. I still have a long way to go; that much I can't deny.

I will keep going.

I will keep grieving.

I will see this thing through, whether it takes two years or four years or every day for the rest of my life. Why? Because if I want to be a whole and healthy person, someone who honors the person God created me to be, then I simply cannot ignore the impact of trauma and suffering. I can't just stuff my grief.

No, we will face it, knowing we have a Companion there in our pain. I pray you do the same.

If you have caught yourself feeling tempted to abandon your beliefs because of the grief you feel, I encourage you not to sustain yet another loss by losing your faith. One of the most important things we can do as we wrestle with grief is to make space to press in and anchor ourselves in truth.

Seasons of terrifying darkness can cause us to question what we said we believed in the light. We can use the hard seasons and the doubts in our faith to drive us deeper into a relentless faith in the good character of God by reminding ourselves time and again of what we find in Scripture. Going to Scripture will not only guide us; it will comfort us as well.

ONE OF THE MOST IMPORTANT THINGS WE CAN DO AS WE WRESTLE WITH GRIEF IS TO MAKE SPACE TO PRESS IN AND ANCHOR OURSELVES IN TRUTH.

I've experienced these moments of doubt myself and know how hard it can be to push into truth when the emotion of the pain is overwhelming. You know, a few days after my sweet nephew Oliver passed away, I slipped into the back of our church, where I knew I would be pointed toward the truth of my Savior. I felt raw and uncertain about rejoining the normal routine of life after witnessing such a colossal loss, so I sat anonymously in the back row. During the time of greeting, one of our pastors shared the simple phrase, "He is faithful."

He is faithful.

God is faithful.

He's faithful today and every day.

Normally when faced with such obvious truth about God, I would reflexively nod my head, grin knowingly, feel a certain settledness in my soul. But on this day, there on the back row, a two-word question wormed its way through my thoughts.

Is he?

In my pain, I was questioning God's faithfulness. Would he be faithful in light of *this*?

In that moment, I didn't want God's faithfulness. I wanted Oliver, alive and well. How could a good God take my sister's baby from her? What a cruel and unjust thing to do.

As I sat through the rest of that service, a curious thing happened to me. In the same way that as soon as you plug a cord into an outlet, power begins to flow, once I sat in God's presence—and amid others who also were longing to encounter someone transcendent and all-knowing and real—my doubts, deep though they were, found their resolution in the certainty that God is not only faithful but also impossibly, immutably *good*.

If you are doubting God today, know that it's okay. God can handle your questions. He can handle your outrage. He can handle your cries of "foul!" His truth is strong enough to absorb the lies that we're tempted to buy when in pain.

Consider that in his goodness, God has made a way to see and understand us in our pain through the cross of Christ where grief, sorrow, and loss connect to hope, love, and joy. Through the cross, God has made a pathway for us to move toward healing. Taking steps forward in our grief, and taking steps to meditate on truth, brings more hope, love, joy, and, ultimately, more of him.

And while I encourage you not to let go of your faith in the grieving process, the process of grief is indeed a process of letting go: letting go of our grasp for control, of wrong beliefs, of what once was, and learning to live in the new reality of life after loss. You will find in yourself the scars from your loss, and life with those scars may feel like a reality you don't want to fit into. But resilience is choosing to show up anyway and find the good, the new, and the beauty that is still to be experienced. It is a choice to begin looking to the now and the future instead of only the past. And in all of it—past, present, and future—we see God with us, his steady hand a constant source of comfort. So hear me in this: even while I advocate for our leaning into grief through lament, please don't stop there. Because the people of Christ's church, with their eyes on the cross, can boldly walk in joy and victory—if not in the current moment of grief, then someday as we continue to point our focus on the hope of Christ for our circumstances.

The grief that Michael and I have faced has provided opportunities to know more of God's character. We've seen his consistency in our loss of control as we look back and glimpse the thread of his faithfulness in both the highs and lows of life. And seen through that lens, navigating grief can be understood as a divine gift in that it has given us a clearer picture of our God's faithfulness.

"Do not let my love turn bitter," I once read in a poignant book titled *Every Moment Holy II* in the chapter "Liturgy for the Loss of a Child":

> Let it turn fierce instead. Fierce in faith, fierce in its resolve to seek first the Kingdom of my God, tenacious in pursuit of that which is eternal, tender in compassion toward the suffering of others, invested in acts of kindness, mercy, creativity, reconciliation, and restoration, convinced that all lost joys mourned in this life are but pale preludes of the fullness to come.[8]

Yes.
That—just that.
Yes and amen to that.

A CHANCE TO COLLECT YOUR THOUGHTS

Sit with your thoughts before God for a few minutes, paying attention to how you're feeling as you read each question to yourself. Take as much time as you need before moving on in the book.

Learning to Lament

1. Has it been true for you that your past seasons of deepest grief align with the seasons when you felt most out of control? What do you make of the correlation or the lack thereof?
2. What do you make of the idea that unaddressed emotional distress can show up in our physical bodies over time?
3. Have you ever intentionally carved out time to lament, to sit with your pain for the purpose of acknowledging it and moving through it? What benefits do you expect you'd receive if you incorporated it more into your life?
4. How carefully, thoroughly, and faithfully do you care for your physical body? How well would those who know you best say that you do?

CHAPTER 5

POWERLESSNESS

Surrendering to God

Our greatest motive for surrendering to him cannot be for what he will do in us. It must be to love him for what he did for us.

—TIMOTHY KELLER

LAUREN

I grew up in a church that would often sing "I Surrender All" in a Sunday morning worship service. It was familiar enough that when I heard the opening piano chords, I started singing the words in my mind before the music director put the microphone to his mouth. Given familiarity, words can often lose their impact. But when I really stop to consider this idea of *freely giving all to Jesus*, the weight of those words in the chorus sinks in.

During the month leading up to the trial that would determine whether Michael and I would be allowed to raise Ezra or whether he would be handed over to the family member who had come forward seeking this boy, our stress level soared. Candidly, surrendering felt like the last thing I wanted to do. Ezra had been with us almost a year, and at most points of his case we thought he would end up being with us forever. Recent revelations about the case had us questioning if Ezra would get to come home to us, causing the whole situation to feel overwhelming—and most certainly beyond our control. There was not a thing Michael or I could do to affect the case. It was solely up to the judge to decide, and we as the adoptive parents weren't considered in the decision-making process at all. So, our role was to parent Ezra and care for him as our own as we had all year while we waited for the system to determine the future of our child.

It was a helpless place to be.

Can't I Control *Something*?

In adoption circles, it's commonly held that a family should wait one full year after adopting a child before pursuing the adoption of another. As Ezra's trial neared, I was in the process of completing the vast quantity of paperwork required to adopt another child.

And while it felt good to busy myself with the tasks of filling out paperwork, making copies of forms, locating records, and double-checking applications, I can see that my fierce drive toward these efforts to grow our family were also rooted in something else: a desire to control something—anything.

If I couldn't control the situation with Ezra, then I would find something else to control. And that's exactly what I did. I finished a new adoption application in a record amount of time for me, and in the midst of holiday parties and Christmas shopping I found time to dot every i and cross every t.

I was in control.

Or trying to be, anyway.

Control—even the illusion of it—brings us comfort. Who wouldn't want control over their circumstances? Why would anyone want to willingly surrender their control? It is human nature to grasp at things we can control. And in our desire to control, we are really tapping into our desire to have power. Power and control go hand in hand. Power is a gift that has been bestowed by God, and power can provide the ability to control with the many forms of influence it brings.[1] But power, like anything else, can become an idol. In those moments our relationship with control needs to shift to one of surrender.

Consider that in Genesis 1, immediately after creating mankind, God provided Adam and Eve with a mandate: "Be fruitful and increase in number; fill the earth and subdue it" (v. 28). From the beginning, man and woman were created with the mandate to steward the power that God had given them, to create and influence people (be fruitful), and to have dominion over the rest of creation.

POWER CAN BECOME AN IDOL. IN THOSE MOMENTS OUR RELATIONSHIP WITH CONTROL NEEDS TO SHIFT TO ONE OF SURRENDER.

The all-powerful Creator created mankind in his image with a mandate to do the very thing the Creator had just done: exercise dominion. In his book titled *Identity and Idolatry*, author Richard Lints observed that paradoxically, the Creator has made human creatures whose very identity has given them power and enables them to move from stewarding such a responsibility to choosing to take advantage of this responsibility because of the power of their will.[2]

Using the power that you possess is often an innate, perhaps subconscious, daily occurrence. You use the power you have through your talents and abilities to create while you're at work. You use your influence in the relationships you have as a parent, spouse, family member, or friend to direct conversation, shape opinions, and draw attention to issues you find important to discuss. You use your financial power to buy things out of necessity or preference. We have power and control over the daily choices we make, and how we use our power in the form of control is largely up to us.

The Power We Seek

It takes power to have control, and if control can bring comfort, we will seek power so that it might provide us comfort and certainty. But is seeking power a bad thing? Money and wealth can be painted in a negative light in some faith circles. After all, the Bible describes the "love of money" as "a root of all kinds of evil" (1 Timothy 6:10). But money in and of itself is not evil; it is the "love of money," the improper ordering of money to the point it attains an idolatrous state in your heart, that can steal our attention from God. Having abundant financial resources can be a great tool when stewarded for the flourishing of others and held in its proper place—not as a god but as a resource to honor God. In the same way, power must be recognized for what it is. Power is not to be idolized but rather stewarded for God's glory and for the flourishing of others.

Power wielded for the sake of having control is not bad in and of itself. Yet it must not be idolized or placed at a higher importance than God but always held in submission to him. Even when held in the proper place, power and control are dangerous if they are not joined with love and vulnerability. For those in Christ, the most extreme application of power and control were stewarded with love and vulnerability when, out of love for his Father's will and for humankind, Jesus willingly didn't exercise his power but instead became vulnerable, nailed nearly naked to a Roman cross to face a gruesome death. In that scene of crucifixion, Jesus would have appeared to be powerless to any onlookers as they saw him in submission to the Roman soldiers who wielded the hammer on those nails that pierced his flesh.

Despite the appearance, Jesus never gave up his power. Throughout the entire crucifixion, Jesus Christ remained firmly in control. He was still fully God, and as such, he still had full access to divine authority. What he did do was lay aside that power for our sake. And then, in complete contrast to the vision of absolute powerlessness and lack of control, Christ showed ultimate power by dying on a cross at the hands of those he created and by conquering the grave when he rose to life again. And in his sacrifice and resurrection, he not only was brought back to life but, in his power, made a way for us to have life in him as well. In love and with vulnerability, God used his power to make a way for us. It is a beautiful picture of stewarding power and control for the sake of God's glory.

> POWER AND CONTROL ARE DANGEROUS IF THEY ARE NOT JOINED WITH LOVE AND VULNERABILITY.

Christ lived and modeled love and vulnerability for the sake of the gospel, which meant that his relationship with power and control was seen through the lens of how he might bring glory to the Father. Following Christ's example from his time on earth means living our lives in a way that reflects how he stewarded his control for God's glory and the good of others.

Reflecting Christ

As believers, we hope to reflect Christ and how he handled power and control. As we trust Christ and rest in our identity as being made in God's image, the way we see ourselves changes. When we understand who we are as image bearers, it gives us a confident self-identity, which results in a willingness to trust in God and steward our power according to his purposes.

On the contrary, the misuse of power shows weakness, not strength. One research study on power recognized a correlation between use of power and identity, noting that whenever people misuse power, they portray a weak self-concept. It is their fragility of personhood that causes them to try to dominate others and to force their will on the world.[3]

Genesis 1 gives us this key to our identity when we see that God created mankind in his image. Having a right view of our image-bearing identity frees us to embrace vulnerability because we can combat the lies we tell ourselves with the truth of who we are in our God-given identity. When we believe in our value as image bearers, it is transformative. One of the ways that right beliefs will impact our lives is in how we connect with power and control. Instead of desiring and grasping at power to control our circumstances, right beliefs will allow us to steward whatever power we do hold, have a healthy relationship with control, and ultimately find rest in knowing the one who holds ultimate control.

Soon after the judge ruled that we would have to release Ezra from our care, I remember wanting to control the narrative about our story with him. Specifically, I felt the need for people to know the depth of our pain. What I feared was that people would say, "Well, just think of your time with Ezra like it was a foster care situation—you know, you were just supposed to have him for a short time."

The fact is, saying goodbye to a child in foster care can be devastating even as you know it is a likely outcome. Plus, our scenario was never intended to be a foster care situation. It had been an adoption plan from the start.

Or I feared people would dismiss my pain and say, "You know, at least Ezra is still alive and well. At least he'll grow up and live his life." As if his being alive should take away the pain of having him completely removed from my life. We have walked alongside friends and family who have experienced the unspeakably difficult road of losing a child who passed away, and while our circumstances are different from theirs, I've often found parallels to the pain they've expressed from no longer having their child. I wanted to control conversations around the loss of our son out of my own fear of the hurtful things that people might say. In all of it I felt very alone.

I do remember feeling a distinct shift in my insecurity about the depth of my grief. It happened four months after we lost Ezra, when some of our closest friends, Landry and Kayla, lost their twin newborn boys. Due to health complications outside their control, our friends had given birth to Simeon and Elias prematurely, and their sons lived only a week before they passed away. The loss of our friends' boys happened so soon after our own loss that it felt as though my grief were fresh all over again.

As Michael preached at the funeral for those two precious boys, I looked around and oddly found comfort and healing to see that there had been space carved out for friends to gather together and mourn their loss. Our own loss was unique since it wasn't a death, and we never had a moment to gather with our loved ones and reflect, cry, lament, and mourn together. Watching our community show up for our friends, carry them, and cry with them in that funeral somehow brought healing in my own heart, knowing that if it had been appropriate, our community would have done the same for our loss.

While I don't want to compare our loss of Ezra to anyone who has lost a child to death, I did find a heartbreaking sense of comfort watching my friends navigate their deepest grief with continued trust in Christ. I sat in Sunday school class with Landry and Kayla, watched them hold to the same truths of God's goodness that I was feebly clinging to, and found I didn't feel so alone. I wasn't the only one grieving a child.

As I processed the ways I had been insecure about my own grief given its unique nature, I saw I was increasingly wrapped up in creating a narrative that would cause others to validate my grief. I was afraid that if people dismissed it (i.e., "Oh, but he didn't die!" or "Well, in adoption you know the risks going into it!"), the depths of my pain would be completely unseen. I needed to be seen in my grief to feel validated in how overwhelming it all was. As I focused on my need for external validation, I became less and less wrapped up in God and more wrapped up in myself. I thought I could control my grief, and that if it was just validated enough, I would somehow feel better about it all. But things never work out when we try to fix things in our own strength, do they?

It would take hours of earnest prayer over many weeks for me to recenter myself in Christ. No amount of external validation was going to soothe the ache I felt in my soul. This would be an inside job. I didn't need earthly validation—I needed Christ.

When you face a circumstance you can't control, it can feel disorienting to realize that you have much less power over your circumstances than you may have previously thought. Yet we can still hold to confidence because in the power of the gospel, we are given the freedom to embrace a Savior who is good and all-powerful. This should give us all the courage in the world to rest more easily in life's vulnerable places, knowing that we are safe in our Father's hands. When our identity is not in our own power and control, we can surrender to the one who is all-powerful, who is in control. We can be honest about our lack of control, knowing that by God's grace we are okay. As we surrender and lean into our vulnerability, we better reflect God and his power and glory.[4]

This is an invitation to consider the areas of our lives where we might be refusing to let go and surrender to what God is doing. To surrender means giving up control and handing it to someone else. It takes active intentionality to release the grip we have on what we think is best for ourselves, for our families, and for our circumstances. It means actively choosing to trust in God and to fully surrender to his plan.

IN THE POWER OF THE GOSPEL, WE ARE GIVEN THE FREEDOM TO EMBRACE A SAVIOR WHO IS GOOD AND ALL-POWERFUL.

Living Surrendered

We can tell ourselves we trust God and that we freely surrender to him, but when we are desperate, our good intentions are put to the test. Certainly, the sudden, unwanted loss of control over a situation in our lives is something that can drive us to feeling desperate. In those days after we said goodbye to Ezra forever, I felt a kind of overwhelming desperation that I'd never experienced before. I would have done anything to have my child back in my arms and sensed myself grasping for something, *anything* I could do to find control in our situation and force things to be the way I wished they were. When feeling the desperation to control a situation or a person, we need to pause and work through our own hesitancy to surrender our circumstance to God.

Years ago, when Michael and I initially started seeing infertility specialists, it felt like we entered a hamster wheel of infertility treatments. We endured labs, questions, more labs, more questions, tests, different doctors, treatment plans, things not working, being directed to more intensive treatment plans, and more. Ironically, as I write this section from a local coffee shop, I can overhear two women sitting behind me talking about infertility. "It feels like I fell into a bottomless black hole," one is saying. "There are so many tests to take, treatments to try, diets to adhere to, activities to avoid . . ."

How I wish I could glance her way with a look that says, "I get it. I've been there too."

For me now, being more than eight years into the infertility journey yet still not achieving a pregnancy, I look back on the journey and see how willing I was to do everything the doctors said to do in hopes of achieving what I desired. I had fully surrendered to the infertility treatment steps, and in a sense, I let them control my life. While it is good to be able to follow a treatment plan, I knew I'd made this one an idol.

When anything in this world has our full surrender instead of God, it does become an idol. My pastor, Rick Thompson, often quotes John Calvin by saying, "The human heart is a perpetual idol factory." Believers resist our heart's natural tendency to find idols when we fill our hearts with Christ. When we seek a robust understanding of who God is in Scripture and surrender to him and what he has done for us in Christ, we surrender to the only thing worthy of our heart's attention.[5]

But surrender to something always requires a denial of other things—a denying of other idols, a denying of our very selves. As Jesus said to his disciples, "Whoever wants to be my disciple must deny themselves and take up their cross daily and follow me" (Luke 9:23). Surrendering to God means we deny the things of this world, and we deny ourselves and our selfish desires. It is choosing to submit to God's authority in our lives.

When Jesus spoke about authority and control, he said, "Very truly I tell you, the Son can do nothing by himself; he can do only what he sees his Father doing, because whatever the Father does the Son also does" (John 5:19). He continued in verse 30: "By myself I can do nothing; I judge only as I hear, and my judgment is just, for I seek not to please myself but him who sent me."

Jesus, the example we are to follow, chose to live in full and complete submission to the Father as he perfectly followed God's will. Jesus lived out that surrender to God's will even to the point of death, essentially saying to his Father, "You do whatever you will do. My life exists in service to you. I am not mine. I am yours."

What Submission Looks Like

In terms of our desire to control things, there are three categories that our circumstances fit into:

- things we have full control over,
- things we have partial control over, and
- things we have no control over.

How we think about surrendering our desires to God will look different depending on what category our circumstance fits into.

I find there are very few things that live in the categories of full control and no control. Most things have varying degrees of partial control. Considering full control first, this is mainly going to be our emotional responses and our personal beliefs. When my young daughter is responding poorly to a directive to put away her toys and clean up, she might yell, "I don't like that!" I often respond by acknowledging that I can see she is sad but reminding her that even if she isn't in control of deciding that it is time to clean up, she is in control of how she responds.

Psychiatrist and Holocaust survivor Viktor Frankl, when reflecting on his time in the Nazi concentration camp Kaufering III, said, "Forces beyond your control can take away everything you possess except one thing, your freedom to choose how you will respond to the situation."[6]

We may not always feel like we have full control over our responses, yet the areas of our lives over which we have the most control are our outlook on life and our response to what happens to us. The single greatest thing that impacts our outlook and response is what we believe. This being the case, it's critical to know what we believe. It's why we must fill ourselves with a knowledge of Scripture, knowing God and his character by what he says about himself in his Word, so that our beliefs are well informed and sturdy in our minds and hearts.

Then there are those areas we have partial control over. Think about your job or your relationships. In your job you likely have some level of control over how things turn out. You can put in the work and do your best, but at the end of the day you don't have control over your employer's decisions, which means you can be laid off. In your relationships, whether in marriage, as a parent, as a neighbor, or as a friend, you can do your part to cultivate a strong bond, but for the relationship to truly thrive, the other person must also act. You have *partial* control, which affects your part, but you'll never have full control.

Finally there are those areas in life we have no control over: natural disasters, economic downturns, a global pandemic, a cancer diagnosis, unexplained infertility, a failed adoption, and more.

As you think about the different areas that you find yourself trying to control, consider which category your circumstance fits into. When we acknowledge how significant or minimal our role is in the outcome of a given situation, that awareness undoubtedly informs our prayers as we seek to surrender time and again to God's will. And surrendering to God's will takes constant practice and intentionality to live a life yielded to him, though the life yielded to our Creator is a life that has room for more peace.

Perhaps one of the more famous prayers in our culture is attributed to Lutheran theologian Reinhold Niebuhr, made popular by the work of Alcoholics Anonymous and its church-based counterpart, Celebrate Recovery. While this prayer has been helpful specifically for those working through addiction, its wisdom applies to us all:

> God grant me the serenity to accept the things I cannot change, courage to change the things I can, and wisdom to know the difference. Living one day at a time, enjoying one moment at a time; accepting hardships as the pathway to peace; taking, as Jesus did, this sinful world as it is, not as I would have it; trusting that You will make all things right if I surrender to Your Will; so that I may be reasonably happy in this life and supremely happy with You forever in the next.[7]

A CHANCE TO COLLECT YOUR THOUGHTS

Sit with your thoughts before God for a few minutes, paying attention to how you're feeling as you read each question to yourself. Take as much time as you need before moving on in the book.

What It (Really) Means to Let God Be God

1. How have you experienced the idea that people who abuse personal power do so because they possess a weak self-concept? Do you think our culture agrees or disagrees with that assertion? Why?
2. When was the last time you realized that having less power over a particular set of circumstances makes more room for you to welcome the gospel's power?
3. If you were to deepen your level of surrender to God—his will, his ways, his power, his peace—what attitudes, habits, and patterns of living might have to be paused for a time?

CHAPTER 6

INTIMACY

The Joy of His Presence

Each time God gives us a hard lesson,
He desires also to give us Himself.
—ELISABETH ELLIOT

MICHAEL

Since the first day I held Zion, I have given her extra hugs and kisses as if attempting to make up for the first nineteen months of her life, when demonstrations of my love were absent from hers. Once she was part of our family and enjoying real food, her cheeks quickly plumped up, providing the perfect landing spot for soft smooches. Her tummy plumped up too, and every time I tickled her there, she'd fall into an avalanche of infectious giggles.

Those first fifty days with Zion were the culmination of years of longing to have the new-parent experiences, but we never could have imagined just how sweet the reality could be. Our parental leave did not involve overseeing a newborn who sleeps twenty-plus hours each day but rather an eighteen-month-old who had seemingly endless energy for engaging with her surroundings and with us. Thankfully, we were well rested. I wouldn't trade those early fully immersed days that centered on going for walks in the neighborhood, strolling through the zoo, and having family come to visit for anything in the world.

As I rocked Zion to sleep at night, I would cradle her with my left arm while placing my right hand on her stomach. Every night I did that. But the memory that stands out most for me is the night before Lauren and I took her to the hospital for her surgery. With my hand resting gently on my child's small body, I realized that mere centimeters below my palm was a tumor that threatened Zion's life. Was it cancerous? Had it spread? Would this be the thing to take her life? We didn't know the answers to any of these questions. All I could do was pray over her, wishing with every fiber of my being that I could take the tumor from her.

I have a video of Zion walking down the hall at Oklahoma Children's Hospital the night before surgery. It is nearly midnight, and no one else is around. As usual, my fun-loving little tot is hobbling down the hall in her pajamas and socks, slipping and falling on her bottom and then laughing each time, oblivious as to why we're there. For all her growing awareness of life, she has no idea what tomorrow holds.

But I know.

So much of parenting is problem-solving. You figure out how to help your child by creating opportunities for growth, by preventing disasters, by kissing scraped elbows and knees. Parents shouldn't have to deal with tumors. Tumors should be deemed out of bounds. Lauren and I knew that we had no hope of curing Zion of this affliction. We had placed 100 percent of our confidence in the hands of medical staff, even as they told us in that certain legally obligated tone, "There are no guarantees."

The anesthesia alone could be fatal, they said as they asked us to verbally confirm that we wanted to proceed.

"What choice do we have?" I remember saying. The answer, as if there could be one, was *no choice*. No choice at all.

I intentionally steered clear of surfing the web after learning my lesson the hard way. Days prior, after having heard the official name of Zion's cancer, I pulled out my phone to run a quick Google search, saw the numbers "45–65%" in a headline, and immediately pocketed it again.

When the time came to take Zion into pre-op, kiss her goodbye, and place her in the arms of a nurse who would take her away, I clung to my daughter, knowing it could be for the last time. As our family and friends watched Lauren and Zion and me walk down the hall where we had played and laughed the night before, Zion looked over my shoulder and offered her adoring support team a heart-melting wave as the three of us marched toward our fate.

Clutching my baby girl tight, I stole a few more sweet cheek kisses. My mind flew through likely scenarios—inoperable tumor, botched surgery, complications nobody foresaw—a carousel spun out of control. *This is futile*, I finally reasoned. *Pick a better thought.*

Then this one came to mind: *I don't know what tomorrow holds, but I know who holds tomorrow.*

The God Who Holds Tomorrow

The reality that God is somehow sovereign over suffering without compromising his goodness is a paradoxical mystery beyond comprehension. Yet the Bible teaches that this is so.

Take the story of Joseph, for example. In the book of Genesis, Joseph was sold into slavery in Egypt by his brothers, who told their father, Jacob, that their younger brother was dead. Joseph was then falsely accused and imprisoned, but eventually—after interpreting the dreams of Pharaoh—he was appointed as second-in-command throughout the land. After the elder brothers were reunited with the one they left for dead, they feared that Joseph might use his power against them. Joseph responded in Genesis 50:20: "You intended to harm me, but God intended it for good to accomplish what is now being done, the saving of many lives."

God not only uses circumstances generated by other people's

sin to be redeemed for good; he somehow *orchestrates the evil* brought into the world by sin to lead to good while still never causing anyone to sin. "When tempted, no one should say, 'God is tempting me,'" James 1:13 says, "for God cannot be tempted by evil, nor does he tempt anyone." So while suffering indeed can show up as a result of our sin, it always shows up so that God's glory can be revealed.

The Bible consistently points to God being sovereign over our suffering. And that is really good news for a few reasons. First, God is just in all his ways, so if he is ordaining difficult things in our lives to come our way, we can trust him, even when we cannot see the full picture. As the apostle Paul said in 1 Corinthians 13:12, "For now we see only a reflection as in a mirror; then we shall see face to face. Now I know in part; then I shall know fully, even as I am fully known." The life of faith is a life of trust. In seasons where we cannot see the wisdom of God working in our life circumstances, we can trust that he is trustworthy because of how he has proven himself in the past.

HIS GOODNESS DOES NOT EBB AND FLOW. IT IS AN ETERNAL STREAM OF RIGHTEOUSNESS FLOWING TO MAKE AND REMAKE ALL THINGS GOOD.

Second, God is good, which means that if something leads to pain, it wasn't because of our sin or Satan's schemes alone. God was working in our sinful hearts and the Enemy's wicked plans to ultimately put the divine glory of the Godhead on display. His goodness does not ebb and flow. It is an eternal stream of righteousness flowing to make and remake all things good. Now, this does *not* mean all things that happen in this sin-stained reality are good. Rather, this truth reminds us that as was the case with Joseph, the worst things that happen to us will one day be turned to good, whether in this reality or the reality to come.

Finally, God is powerful. His strength is not limited by life's circumstances. Though the forces of darkness throw their worst at us, not a hair on our heads is harmed apart from the providential hand of almighty God ordaining it to be so. He cannot be outworked, outgunned, or outmatched. He gave life to everything that exists and is himself holding all things together. Therefore, we can know that whatever comes our way is intentionally given to us by a God who has the power to direct our destiny.

Where God Is When He Seems Far Away

The beauty of Christianity is that it is not a religion where you work to make right your wrongs. Rather, Jesus does that for you, and you receive a relationship with him that becomes your salvation and your joy. The intimacy God offers is the most compelling thing about our faith.

This also means we recognize our powerlessness to change our experience with God by our own effort. We are dependent on his mercy not only to receive our pardon but also to experience his presence. Indeed, some of the most impassioned words in all of Scripture involve someone who loved God but also felt as if our heavenly Father was far off, as if God had abandoned him. I think of David's words in Psalm 61: "From the ends of the earth I call to you, I call as my heart grows faint; lead me to the rock that is higher than I" (v. 2). Or how about David praying to God in Psalm 13: "How long, Lord? Will you forget me forever? How long will you hide your face from me? How long must I wrestle with my thoughts and day after day have sorrow in my heart? How long will my enemy triumph over me?" (vv. 1–2). David wasn't really expecting an answer to his opening question; his theology being sound, he knew that God doesn't abandon his people. But in that moment his emotions did not reflect what his mind knew was true. His despair was so deep that his disillusionment and grief had no choice but to erupt: *Are you going to leave me here in this pit forever?*

Author and pastor Philip Yancey once said,

> I have learned one absolute principle in calculating God's presence or absence, and that is that I cannot. God, invisible, sovereign, who according to the psalmist "does whatever pleases him," sets the terms of the relationship. I cannot control such a God. At best I can put myself in the proper frame to meet him. I can confess sin, remove hindrances, purify my life, wait expectantly, and—perhaps hardest of all—seek solitude and silence. I offer no guaranteed method to obtain God's presence, for God alone governs that.[1]

To borrow a lesson from chapter 5, to experience the presence of God is something you have only partial control over at best. You cannot force the hand of the Almighty by your own might. All you can do is ask for mercy to trust him in the desert and treaure him when the rain comes.

Last year I was part of the teaching team that led our church through a series on the Psalms, and each time I prepared a message from that book of the Bible, I was struck afresh by how often the various psalmists—David, of course, but also Moses,

Solomon, Asaph, and others—lashed out at God rhetorically or at least begged him for relief:

> Why, LORD, do you stand far off? Why do you hide yourself in times of trouble? (10:1)

> Listen to my words, LORD, consider my lament. (5:1)

> O God, why have you rejected us forever? Why does your anger smolder against the sheep of your pasture? (74:1)

> I am worn out from my groaning. All night long I flood my bed with weeping and drench my couch with tears. (6:6)

> My God, my God, why have you forsaken me? Why are you so far from saving me, so far from my cries of anguish? My God, I cry out by day, but you do not answer, by night, but I find no rest. (22:1–2)

Eventually we come to the end of our self-fueled strength. We run after our deepest desire as long as humanly possible but are ultimately forced to resign ourselves to the outcome we wanted least. Deflated and defeated, we have nowhere else to turn but to abject hopelessness—or to the waiting arms of God.

DEFLATED AND DEFEATED, WE HAVE NOWHERE ELSE TO TURN BUT TO ABJECT HOPELESSNESS—OR TO THE WAITING ARMS OF GOD.

Elisabeth Elliot was the wife of missionary Jim Elliot, who was killed in 1956 by the very Waodani people that he and four of his friends had traveled thousands of miles to serve. The Waodani were known to be violent, especially to outsiders, so the missionaries spent months flying over their village and dropping gifts before finally landing on a nearby riverbank and setting up camp.

After one peaceful visit by three of the Waodani, Jim and his friends radioed to their families to pray for them as they anticipated another visit soon. But the next day a group of Waodani speared all five men, believing them to be cannibals. Several days later a search party found several of their bodies at the campsite and one in the nearby river. Jim Elliot was twenty-eight years old when he died, survived by his incredulous young wife, Elisabeth, and their sole child—a daughter named Valerie.

The Elliots' legacy to this day is one of unwavering faithfulness to God. Still, wouldn't you and I both forgive them for raising a fist toward the heavens and demanding answers at once—Jim as he sustained that first wretched blow, and Elisabeth as she was made to endure the next six decades separated from the person she loved most?

No question Elisabeth had seasons like the psalmists, who wrestled with the "why" during their challenges, yet she endured tragic loss and grew stronger by building her life on the bedrock of the sovereignty of God over life. She rejected the idea that her suffering was random, and she didn't accept the idea God was unloving because he didn't spare her suffering. "We're not adrift in chaos. We're held in the everlasting arms," she later wrote. "And therefore, and this makes a difference, we can be at peace, and we can accept. We can say yes, Lord, I'll take it. The faculty by which I apprehend God is the faculty of faith."[2]

I know it's difficult to believe when we're neck-deep in the throes of grief, but in terms of where God is when we're suffering, the answer is *right here, holding us tight*. We know this because of the apostle Paul's words in Romans 8:32, where he says that God "did not spare his own Son, but gave him up for us all." Christianity offers to us a God who does not stand apart from our pain but rather has entered our world and taken on the most agonizing physical torment of the crucifixion *and* the most excruciating spiritual agony of the wrath of God poured out. The gospel message centers on the fact that instead of remaining in the comforts of heaven surrounded by the love of God and the fellowship of the Holy Spirit, Jesus left paradise to make a way for us to be brought into the presence of God. He left his comfort to make a way for us to be comforted. He took on God's wrath so we could receive God's mercy. If not for the suffering of Christ, we would never experience intimacy with God.

So often God answers our own cries for help "not by explaining his providence," wrote Ligon Duncan in his magnificent work on suffering, *When Pain Is Real and God Seems Silent*, "but by giving us a deeper understanding of his person."[3] It's an understanding reserved for those who even on the darkest of days choose wholeheartedly to trust in him and, in doing so, allow pain to be a pathway toward greater intimacy with God.

God's Good Goal for Our Lives

Since the beginning of time, as recounted in the book of Genesis, God has demonstrated a pattern of creating to bring glory to himself through that created thing. He created the heavens, and according to Psalm 19:1, those heavens "declare the glory of God; the skies proclaim the work of his hands." As part of that creation, he made humankind. Genesis 1:27–28 says, "So God created mankind in his own image, in the image of God he created them; male and female he created them. God blessed them and said to them, 'Be fruitful and increase in number; fill the earth and subdue it. Rule over the fish in the sea and the birds in the sky and over every living creature that moves on the ground.'"

And why were we created? In the apostle Paul's letter to the church at Ephesus, he wrote that "in him we were also chosen, having been predestined according to the plan of him who works out everything in conformity with the purpose of his will, in order that we, who were the first to put our hope in Christ, might be for the praise of his glory" (Ephesians 1:11–12).

Here's what that means: Despite cultural opinions to the contrary, the whole reason for our existence is to live to the praise of God's glory, in times of delight *and* despair. God did not need us, as we so often assume of the people who matter in our lives. He was complete before any created thing came to be. Yet in his lavish mercy, and for his pleasure, he created us. "You are worthy, our Lord and God, to receive glory and honor and power, for you created all things, and by your will they were created and have their being," John wrote in Revelation 4:11.

When we enter a personal relationship with God by confessing his Son as Lord, we cede control of our lives to him—to his will, to his ways, to his plan. The apostle Paul said it this way in Galatians 2:20: "I have been crucified with Christ and I no longer live, but Christ lives in me. The life I now live in the body, I live by faith in the Son of God, who loved me and gave himself for me."

We are united with God through Christ, brought close to him through the forgiveness of our sin. Because of this truth, we now have access to divine resources that previously were unavailable to us. We who inhabit the natural world now have supernatural power. What this means is that lives that were once marked by chaos can be marked by order. Lives that were once marked by deception can be marked by truth. Lives that were once marked by emotional tailspins can be marked by inexplicable peace. If this seems hard to believe, it's because it is hard to believe! It is a work of God alone. But when we let God work on our behalf, life actually starts to work.

To access these supernaturally stimulated realities, we must keep close to the Giver of those good gifts. And to keep close to him is to acknowledge that even the strongest among us can't retain control or go it alone in life. We were created by him to find our completeness in him. Loss reminds us of this agonizing need.

The Need Behind All Other Needs

After Ezra left, Lauren and I were inundated with emails, greeting cards, flowers, and books with heartfelt personalized inscriptions from friends wishing us comfort and patience and peace. One book we acquired in this season was by theology professor Jerry Sittser called *A Grace Disguised*, in which he recounted the horrific day he simultaneously lost his mother, his wife, and his four-year-old daughter in a car accident. If a single event could render a person's faith null and void, it was probably that one. But this wasn't Jerry's experience. The loss changed him. But it carved out *more* capacity for God, not less.

He wrote,

> Deep sorrow often has the effect of stripping life of pretense, vanity, and waste. It forces us to ask basic questions about what is most important in life. Suffering can lead to a simpler

> life, less cluttered with nonessentials. It is wonderfully clarifying. That is why many people who suffer sudden and severe loss often become different people. They spend more time with their children or spouse, express more affection and appreciation to their friends, show more concern for other wounded people, give more time to a worthy cause, or enjoy more of the ordinariness of life.[4]

I came to those words and reflexively nodded. While I was still spun out over Ezra's departure, I could see Sittser's themes peeking through in my own life. I considered the type of father I'd chosen to be with Zion—and with Ezra while he was in our fold: intentional, present, tuned in. But here's the thing: I don't think I could have gotten there on my own. With hindsight on my side—and after swimming in the deep end of research for this book—I can see that it was the loss itself that catalyzed the change I needed, because that loss is what drove me to God. My deep disappointment in not being able to keep Ezra is what reoriented me to my desperate need for God. The pain that drove me closer to my heavenly Father was also making me a better earthly father to the child who was still in my care.

ONLY GOD CAN FILL THE VOID IN A HUMAN HEART.

It's an odd thing to consider but is true nonetheless: whatever it is we think we need, our need for Jesus stands behind that thing. Only God can fill the void in a human heart. The question is whether we will pursue the created things that lead to emptiness or the Creator who leads to fulfillment (Romans 1:21–25).

In Moses' sermon series known as the book of Deuteronomy,

the great prophet was nearing his death. Before he left the earth, he needed to pass on a set of key reminders to the nation of Israel so that they would be set up for success. He didn't want them to dishonor God. He wanted to beckon them toward obedience. Even so, he recognized that, left to their own human devices, there was no way they would keep the law. During one part of his talk, he warned them against idolatry, explaining that if they decided to start worshiping things made of wood and stone, God's punishment would be swift. "The LORD will scatter you among the peoples, and only a few of you will survive among the nations to which the LORD will drive you," Moses wrote. "There you will worship man-made gods of wood and stone, which cannot see or hear or eat or smell" (Deuteronomy 4:27–28).

This sounds like bad news, right? Unrelenting, punishing, harsh.

But read verse 29: "If from there you seek the LORD your God, you will find him if you seek him with all your heart and with all your soul."

How can we have confidence that God will be found when we are incapable of seeking him with *all* our heart and soul? Because finding God is not dependent on our determination or purity. *God seeks us.* Israel would wander from God, but he would use calamity to turn the hearts of his people back toward himself, as he intends to do with the hardships we face in our lives today. In the climactic demonstration of God's radical never-giving-up love, Jesus came to seek and to save the lost. And boy did we need it. Even at our very best we could never find God on our own any more than we could keep the Law. The Law is meant to act as a mirror in our lives to reveal our dependency on God so that, as Pastor Matt Chandler said, "we might fling ourselves on the one who can and find his grace sufficient for us in the struggle."[5]

It is through brokenness that intimacy with God is built. Jesus at the cross received the wrath from God that we deserved. Why? So that we could receive the mercy from God that he deserved. God's love for you is radical. You, reader. Not a theoretical person. *You. Me.* Our joy is possible only because of his sorrow. Our hope is available only because Jesus denied help. Our lives will be marked with suffering, but we can experience the joy of the comfort of the Holy Spirit and a certainty of our future in his glory.

IT IS THROUGH BROKENNESS THAT INTIMACY WITH GOD IS BUILT.

To follow Jesus is to march toward the cross. Our life's end is an execution. And that execution happened two thousand years ago. So we do not mourn as though at a funeral. We rejoice as though at a wedding. For we have already been crucified and our life is no longer our own. In the midst of trials, we are blessed. The comfort that comes through the power of the Holy Spirit is greater than the worst this life can present.

I don't know what difficulty you face as you read this today. But I hope this truth is an anchor for your soul as it has been to us: not only does God have a plan to use our sorrows for the good of joyful intimacy with him, but he did not spare Jesus himself from suffering. Do not lose heart. Do not place your hope in changing worldly circumstances. Our true hope is in a God who is not only intentional with the suffering he ushers into our lives but who himself has also suffered. One day we will stand before him and our wounds will be healed by his.

A CHANCE TO COLLECT YOUR THOUGHTS

Sit with your thoughts before God for a few minutes, paying attention to how you're feeling as you read each question to yourself. Take as much time as you need before moving on in the book.

Where Is God When It Hurts?

1. Have you ever faced a set of circumstances that transformed the idea, "I don't know what tomorrow holds, but I know who holds tomorrow" from being a cliché to being a lifeline? What was going on at the time? How did the perspective shift help?
2. How is your perception of God's goodness affected by understanding that he not only allows evil into our lives but also *orchestrates* it?
3. When have you come to see God use truly terrible circumstances to bring about good in your life?

CHAPTER 7

PRAYER

Bending Our Will Toward God's

Lament is a prayer in pain that leads to trust.

MARK VROEGOP

LAUREN

For months leading up to Ezra's court date, I had prayed that our family of four would stay intact while also immediately praying that God's will and God's best for Ezra would be done. It was painful to imagine that God's plan might not involve us continuing as Ezra's parents. Nonetheless, I made myself pray for God's will, trusting that he knew best. That was at least what my prayer had been in the lead-up to Ezra's court date. Now here we were, on decision day, and I wavered in my faith.

Sitting on a bench outside of the courtroom with a wall separating me from where a judge would determine the fate of who would parent Ezra, I stared at the court building's marbled pink wall and dark brown trim, and I could no longer bring myself to pray for God's will to be done.

I wanted *my* will.

I wanted my son.

Ezra's case was complicated, and at the end of the day, it could have gone either way. I knew that I had been caring for him to the best of my ability since we brought him home from the hospital twelve months earlier, and I couldn't imagine life without him.

How could it have been better for him to have lost the only home he'd ever known? The only sister he'd ever known? Our extended family that had loved him so well? His church family that had fully embraced him as one of their own?

The closer we got to this possible outcome, the more desperate I became to control that outcome. I knew there was nothing I could do to affect the judge's decision. So I changed the only thing I knew I could change; I decided to change my prayer: *God, I want Ezra to stay with us. Amen.*

I had been praying to bend my will toward God's. Now I was seeking to bend his will toward mine.

Pain Points

Wherever we lack control, there is pain. Whether it is the death of a loved one, a diagnosis we didn't expect, a financial hardship, a sudden job loss, or even the day-to-day challenges of parenting a child who won't comply (do I need to remind you I am still parenting a five-year-old?), you and I both have been there. And when we are in that out-of-control place, feeling the sting of loss and suffering, there is no better place to turn than to the loving Father who has all control.

If you are following the progression of thinking at the end of that previous paragraph, you may be piecing together in your mind the question about God's goodness. After all, if you just went through this painful experience and lack of control, but God has all control, then is he still good that he allowed you this pain? It is a good question. A logical question. One that I've certainly come back to wrestle with, replaying it repeatedly like a song you can't get out of your head.

Take a step back from the pain. God is the Creator of all things. He is the Creator of the universe and of you. God sees all things, from beginning to end. Wouldn't he, in all his wisdom, know how best to care for me and you, even if that plan involves pain? A good parent knows that hard decisions and discipline will shape a young child into a (hopefully) successful adult. As God's children, we should expect that we also will be walking through painful and formative experiences in our lives. And that God, our loving parent, will see us through.

Hardship is a part of life. Satan is at work in our world, and the reality of sin affects us daily. Consider the effects of our fallen world on our bodies alone. If you are over the age of thirty, and you've ever experienced a micro-injury because you've slept wrong and woken up with your back or neck out of whack, I don't have to remind you that in a fallen world, everything is decaying—most acutely, our bodies.

Yet God is sovereign. He is sovereign over Satan, over our lives, over our circumstances, and over all things. Nothing happens that God did not know about and providentially orchestrate or allow. God is also just and holy. As Jackie Hill Perry says in her book *Holier Than Thou*, "If God is holy, then He can't sin. If God can't sin, then He can't sin against me. If He can't sin against me, shouldn't that make Him the most trustworthy being there is?"[1]

Her words are true, even if challenging to live out. When we're stuck in a pit of pain, we may feel angry at God or question his character. It's okay to wrestle through the questions and doubt, and in fact it is a normal progression in the grief process. But as we progress, we can go to God in prayer as a way of relinquishing our grasp at control, as we offer everything over to a good and trustworthy Father—even if we don't feel like it at the time.

The Role of Emotions

For believers, as we experience deep emotions, it is important to remember that our emotions don't have to control us. Emotions inform us—that is absolutely the case. But they need not hold us captive by commanding our thoughts and actions.

Letting your emotions rule you will often lead to greater heartache and despair. Like when I've responded to someone in my anger and said something I wished I hadn't. Or when I've allowed myself to give way to emotional jealousy and bitterness because a friend found out she was pregnant without even trying, while I've walked through years of infertility. As I give way to my negative emotion, I rob myself of the joy and relational connection of celebrating with a friend.

Emotions should inform me, helping me to connect with why I might feel sad about not having a child or mad at someone who hurt me, but I shouldn't be ruled by those emotions. As you wrestle with your emotions, go to God in prayer with them. Prayer often precedes our belief of what we know to be good and true but don't yet feel.

As was mentioned in our chapter on grief, our emotions do have a place and should be validated. Well-informed emotions that are disciplined by the truth of Scripture and reason can be helpful teachers that provide greater insights regarding our own lives and regarding God. When stewarded well, emotions can play a healthy role in our lives, serving as a reminder of our humanity and of our capacity to love. Sadness after loss is an indicator of the deep love we felt. Yet the more time we spend navel-gazing at our own emotional and circumstantial state, the more we will be led to despair. It is good to practice self-reflection, but to find real hope and healing, we must look up and focus on Jesus. As Mark

Vroegop reminds us in *Dark Clouds, Deep Mercy*, "The promise for Christians is as glorious as it is deep: Jesus bought the right to make everything right."[2]

If Christ is our hope because he is the one who can make all things right, we only help ourselves when we look to him. Fixing our eyes on Jesus means choosing *not* to fix our eyes on the things of this world and its comforts—food, pleasure, relationships, adventure, numbing, comparison, self-pity, or any other thing we might turn to instead of our Creator God.

During my darkest seasons of grief, the choice to come to God, pray to God, and trust God to provide the hope I so desperately needed wasn't a reflexive, instantaneous one. It was a *process*. It meant I continued to put myself in an environment where I would be reminded—by his Word, by his church, by others—of God's truth. It took time. As those reminders of God and his magnanimity and glory were placed in front of me, I couldn't help but turn from my own pain and marvel at the incredible character of God. As I reflected on God and connected with him, the reminders helped bring me through the darkest seasons.

One way to look up to God and allow our hearts to believe in the truth of his character is by having conversations with him. We fellowship with God through prayer. God beckons us, saying, "Come to me." The Creator of the universe, who created us in his image, who knit us together in our mother's womb, who sacrificed his Son for our sake, also invites us to come to him when we are heavy laden, and he will lift that weight. "Come to me, all you who are weary and burdened," Jesus said in Matthew 11:28, "and I will give you rest."

I love that passage. It is such a gentle invitation. Have you ever had a friend offer you support such as this? Surely, they cared about you enough to see you in your trouble and want to help.

Similarly, our God sees us, and he invites us to come to him and receive divine rest.

The rest of Matthew 11 is equally compelling. Looking at the context of the chapter a bit deeper, it opens with John the Baptist in prison, sending his messengers to meet with Jesus and ask the other disciples about Jesus' deeds. John seemed to be questioning the divinity of his Messiah, asking Jesus, "Are you the one who is to come, or should we expect someone else?" (v. 3). Jesus did not rebuke John for doubting him. Instead, Jesus reminded his followers of John the Baptist's key role: "Truly I tell you, among those born of women there has not risen anyone greater than John the Baptist; yet whoever is least in the kingdom of heaven is greater than he" (v. 11). Jesus met John the Baptist's doubts with grace and love.

John, who had Jesus with him in the flesh, lacked enough faith at times. Jesus would have known that in the not-too-distant future, John would end up being martyred for his faith. Jesus didn't see John for his doubt. Jesus knew the fruit that would carry forth in John's life until the end, even with moments of doubt and questioning in the mix.

To bring this to a modern-day example, maybe you are walking through one of those seasons where the bottom has just fallen out in your life. You may typically be a positive and upbeat person, but you can't seem to find anything to be cheery about when you look at the landscape of your life. Your family is challenging, work is a nightmare, friendships are waning, the bank account is dwindling, and there is no bright spot to be found. In that environment, you question God and what he is doing: *Is this really how life is going to go?*

John the Baptist would understand. He was there. As he sat in prison, hearing about what was going on outside of those prison cell walls, he wondered if Jesus was the one to come or if there would be another. In light of his circumstances, he doubted what he knew to be true about Jesus. Keep in mind that this was John the Baptist, the very person who leapt in his mother's womb when Jesus was near him in Mary's womb (Luke 1:41). John the Baptist, forerunner of the Messiah, the one who himself baptized Jesus and saw the dove descend on Christ (Matthew 3:13–17). Yet now he questioned it all.

It is with that context of John's doubt that Jesus offered those powerful words from Matthew 11:28–29: "Come to me, all who labor and are heavy laden, and I will give you rest. Take my yoke upon you, and learn from me, for I am gentle and lowly in heart, and you will find rest for your souls" (ESV).

I am grateful that God invites us to come to him even in our doubt. He calls us to be in relationship with him, for he alone can provide rest for our souls. Prayer is our drawing near to God in fellowship, bringing our hearts before him, seeking him, listening to him, simply having presence with him. God is there. He sees, he knows, he hears, and he loves us.

Prayer is a way to merge our theology with our emotions as we enjoy an actual encounter with God. Through prayer we come before God, reminding ourselves of what we know is true, while also allowing ourselves to be honest and cry out to our heavenly Father. This experiential praying requires us to know both

THROUGH PRAYER WE COME BEFORE GOD, REMINDING OURSELVES OF WHAT WE KNOW IS TRUE, WHILE ALSO ALLOWING OURSELVES TO BE HONEST AND CRY OUT TO OUR HEAVENLY FATHER.

Scripture and ourselves through self-reflection. As Timothy Keller reminded us in his book *Prayer*, the discipline of prayer always leads us to deeper intimacy with God.[3]

But we must submit ourselves to the discipline if we want to realize those results. Jesus certainly took time to find solitude and talk to his Father in every season of life, but one of the most detailed accounts of Jesus praying is in a season of anguish. When Jesus went to the garden of Gethsemane with his disciples before he was to be arrested and taken to the cross, he prayed. Jesus asked his disciples to pray as well, but they did not feel the weight of what was about to happen the way Jesus did, and they fell asleep. They were not motivated to push past the distractions or disinterest and focus on prayer. Jesus was left by himself praying. Matthew 26:39 tells us what he prayed for: "Going a little farther, he fell with his face to the ground and prayed, 'My Father, if it is possible, may this cup be taken from me. Yet not as I will, but as you will.'"

Our Will Versus God's

Unlike me, when I shifted my prayers toward my own self-focused will, Jesus held on to the prayer—that God's will would be done—all the way to the end of his life. Christ did for me what I couldn't do for myself—what none of us can do for ourselves. He remained faithful and perfect throughout his whole life, and when he died on the cross, he was the perfect sacrifice that took on the wrath for our sin. Throughout his life and ministry Jesus was unique in his prayer life in this way: every single time Jesus prayed, he referred to God as "Father." Every time except one: during his final prayer, on the cross, when Jesus cried out, "My

God, my God, why have you forsaken me?" (Matthew 27:46). Christ willingly laid down his control and endured the cross, for the sake of you and me and to glorify his Father. Even amid his deepest pain, Christ went to his Father in prayer and surrendered to God's will.

Our own lack of control, our pain, our longing, or our anguish can often lead us in two directions: we will either run to our Father or run away from him. Jesus ran to his Father with full honesty yet also full submission. Jesus acknowledged his desire and voiced it to God yet still accepted that God's will was best. Jesus released his own control over his circumstances to take up God's plan for his life, because even if it did bring him pain, he knew it was ultimately the best choice.

As we go to God in prayer, it helps to remember the character of the one we are praying to. Based on the testimony of Scripture, we know that God is a present Father, a loving Father, a faithful Father, a Father who is good. Who wouldn't want to talk with someone like that?

Michael is currently reading C. S. Lewis's Chronicles of Narnia series to Zion at night before bed. In *The Lion, the Witch and the Wardrobe* Lewis offered an exchange between one of the children who has entered the magical land of Narnia, a young girl named Susan, and a certain Mr. Beaver, a longtime resident of the place. Susan is nervous about meeting Aslan, the lion most readers believe represents God. "Ooh," said Susan. "Is he—quite safe? I shall feel rather nervous about meeting a lion." To which Mr. Beaver replies, "Who said anything about safe? 'Course he isn't safe. But he's good. He's the King, I tell you."[4]

In our own lack of control, our pain, our wrestling, it may not feel like God is a good God to have allowed hard things in our lives. But God is the God of all things; he sees in his providence the way all things will work together. So even while things do not feel safe, we can know that God is still good, and we can go to him.

In Psalm 23, David admitted his own lack of control with the simple statement "The LORD is my shepherd" (v. 1). Sheep are quite helpless, and the psalmist seems to admit his own helplessness and his need for a shepherd in this simple opening statement to this famous psalm. Looking at the New Testament, we see this shepherd-and-sheep analogy being developed when Jesus referred to himself as "the good shepherd" (John 10:11).

Interestingly, while sheep possess the freedom to roam around, grazing where they wish and wandering the pasture, but ultimately, sheep are where they are because the shepherd has led them there. God is our shepherd, and he lovingly cares for us. When we prayerfully release our attempts at control and accept the truth of God's full control and goodness, as John 8:32 reminds us, "then you will know the truth, and the truth will set you free."

Fellowship with Others

As we run to God in prayer even from there in our pain, we convey to a watching world in need that our Father is faithful to heal us. By opening ourselves up and asking for prayer from our friends and those close to us, it allows others to enter into prayer together with us. And in my own experience, I believe it was the prayers of others that gave me strength.

One Sunday during Zion's chemotherapy treatment, when we would normally be at church, I was home with my girl. Her lowered immune system caused us to be in a quarantine phase, so I opted to watch the service online. That morning my pastor, through tears, shared about our situation and encouraged people to pray. I was so touched by the love and support of my church family that to this day the memory gives me pause.

When I was weak, the people God placed in my life were there to stand beside me. I haven't always been good at stepping in to provide that same support to others in their time of need, often because I didn't know what to do. But going through our challenges taught me how much the gift of presence matters. As you lean into fellowship with God, lean also into the community of believers.

We are made for connection, both with our Creator God and with each other. We all have relational needs as humans created in the image of a relational triune God. We have a responsibility to lean into our relationship with God and then also build relationships with others. It takes intentionality, work, and sacrifice.

AS YOU LEAN INTO FELLOWSHIP WITH GOD, LEAN ALSO INTO THE COMMUNITY OF BELIEVERS.

People can often go in one of two different directions in their pain. They can either run to people and relationships instead of God, or they can run from people altogether and seek isolation. For those most likely to run to your friends and relationships in painful seasons, the challenge can become remembering to connect with God first instead of relying only on earthly connection. For those who may trend in the opposite direction and lean toward isolation in seasons of difficulty, we must remember the significance of turning to and leaning on the healthy relationships God has given us.

Attachment is another way of saying "connection." If a child has a strong attachment with their parent or caregiver, it means they are strongly connected with that person. We each have different attachment styles, and our attachment capacity is built when we are children by how we experienced connection with our caregivers.[5]

For children who experience the pain of loss early in life or have some event that breaks the attachment they've had with a parent, it can cause an inability to maintain strong connection with others later in life. A pain point in the child's past keeps them from accessing connection in their future. In a comparable way, as we experience pain in life, our instinct may be to protect ourselves by closing off connection with others. We hide from God and others to avoid any more pain. In the process, we lose connections. But we need connection, we need fellowship, by first running to God and then including our biblical community.

Turning to God and Others

In a faith-based behavioral recovery program used in our church and in churches across the country called Celebrate Recovery, the first step to take toward healing is to admit that you are not God. The second step is to admit that there is a God. This powerful pair acknowledges our own lack of being God, our own lack of control over all things, while pointing to the fact that there is someone who is all-powerful.

In the recovery program it is understood that there is great power in these foundational truths. There is a lesson here for us as well, whether we're recovering from addiction or not. Our own admission of who is in control (God) can bring us peace, the peace to go before him.

You may be wondering, *If I'm going to trust God and go to*

him in prayer, how do I even do that, especially if I don't feel like it or know where to start?

I've found in my own prayer life, the hardest time for me to turn to prayer is during the crisis, when I don't feel like I have the words. There is a type of pain that leaves us at a loss for anything to say. I found comfort knowing that "in the same way, the Spirit helps us in our weakness. We do not know what we ought to pray for, but the Spirit himself intercedes for us through wordless groans" (Romans 8:26).

I have also been a longtime adherent of prayer journaling, and as someone who logs her prayers daily, I rely on having the words to write. Since I was a teenager, I've written prayers and prayer requests in a journal every evening after I read the Bible. I've found that journaling my prayers helps me to focus a specific moment of my day on talking to God.

Reflecting on that Romans 8:26 passage, I've never felt the power of that promise that God's Spirit is interceding for us more personally than when I was trying to pray in those days immediately following the loss of Ezra. The Holy Spirit helps us when we don't have the words; he is there as a comforter; he gives us wisdom and intercedes for us when we can't ourselves. What a gift.

In the days and weeks following our loss of Ezra, in the pain, the words were hard to come by, and in their place were only tears. I knew that even in my own lack of oratory abilities, my God knew and was receiving my nonverbalized prayers.

December 17: *God, I can't believe we lost our son.*
December 18: *God, help.*
December 19: *It hurts so much. God, be with Ezra.*
December 20: *God, this is painful to move forward in life without our son.*

My prayer journal entries above, on the day we lost Ezra—December 17—and in the days following, were brief. Most of them were not much more than the sentences listed above and the dried tearstains on the page. How do you come up with words when facing such pain? The loss seemed to drain every bit of energy or motivation to be able to make it through the day, let alone come up with eloquent prayers or even string together a single sentence. But God was with me in those moments, in my inability and grief.

For years, journaling my prayers has provided a way for me to look back on what I had been praying for during certain seasons of my life. In my journals, I can see God's faithfulness to answer various requests, even if it was in a way I didn't expect. Journaling can be a healthy way to process your thoughts in a safe space, and I found that the journaling process helps me in my prayer time.

I also found looking at the prayers of others to be helpful when I didn't have the capacity to find the right words to pray. I looked at the book of Psalms, and I would cling to passages such as Psalm 34:18: "The Lord is close to the brokenhearted and saves those who are crushed in spirit."

But truthfully, sometimes there are no words. I think about a dream that my sisters and I shared regarding all becoming mothers at the same time, and how Lindy's recent loss of her baby, Oliver, has dashed that dream—from our perspective, anyway. What do we do when the ache of our reality is a world away from the life we thought we would live?

We come to our Father in humble submission. We shoot straight. We tell him what hurts.

As you turn to the promises of who our good Father is and trust him with your prayers, I encourage you to consider ways that you can grow in your prayer life. Whether it be journaling or reading other people's prayers, setting aside a particular time of the day, or carving out space for a dedicated prayer retreat, however it looks for you, disciplining yourself to pray will always deepen your intimacy with God.

A CHANCE TO COLLECT YOUR THOUGHTS

Sit with your thoughts before God for a few minutes, paying attention to how you're feeling as you read each question to yourself. Take as much time as you need before moving on in the book.

The Role of Divine Conversation in Surviving Pain

1. What did you make of the assertion that "when we are in that out-of-control place, feeling the sting of loss and suffering, there is no better place to turn than to the loving Father who has all control"? Do you consider God to be a loving Father? Why or why not?
2. During this season of your life, how are you experiencing the idea that in a fallen world, "everything is decaying"?
3. Describe a time when letting your emotions rule you has led to heartache and despair. What were the circumstances involved? What emotions were in play?
4. Have you ever accepted Jesus' invitation, "Come to me, all you who are weary and burdened, and I will give you rest"? If so, what were the results of your saying yes?

CHAPTER 8

HOPE

Walking Toward the Win

Here is the comfort for every sufferer:
hope is a person, and his name is Jesus.
—PAUL DAVID TRIPP

LAUREN

In 2017 my parents formally opened the doors to one of the most significant accomplishments of their lives, the Museum of the Bible. Located just two blocks from the National Mall in Washington, DC, it is perfectly positioned to attract the millions of tourists who flow through our nation's capital each year, and being one of the largest museums in the DC metro area, it has plenty of exhibits to keep guests enthralled, not just for an hour or two but, if they're so inclined, for days.

Both Michael and I were on staff with the museum during the two years leading up to its grand opening in Washington and thus spent a fair amount of time educating ourselves on the museum's artifacts, promoting its value to donors and guests, and, frankly, just roaming its construction site, imagining the exhibits and being amazed like anyone else by the magnitude of the Bible's impact throughout history and the world.

One of the aspects of the museum that surprises people is how technologically advanced the exhibits are. There are screens everywhere, and peppered throughout the six floors are displays enhanced by audio and video segments, virtual reality, projection mapping, and digital panoramas. It's pretty incredible. But of all the cool things there, one of my favorites has always been the room that showcases real-time searches of the Bible, courtesy of a collaboration with the YouVersion Bible app, the most downloaded Bible app in the world. The exhibit is called the Bible

Now, and at any time of any day you can walk inside and see which Bible verses people are searching for and reading right then, in more than one thousand versions of the Bible and in more than one thousand languages. My data-loving heart always swells when I'm in that room.

I bring all this up to make the following point: Based on those hyper-current, state-of-the-art capabilities, it was plain to spot an interesting trend that started to unfold over the last several years. When Michael would give museum tours back in 2017, 2018, and 2019, he made a habit of pulling up the "view by country" feature on the exhibit and then would type in "US." Without fail, the most popular verse that was being highlighted or shared at that moment would be something about how strong and powerful we are as believers, something like Philippians 4:13, which says, "I can do all things through him who strengthens me" (ESV).

Next, Michael would pull up a country on the other side of the world where one of our missionary friends serves, someplace where the gospel is illegal, and invariably the most popular verses being searched there would be about trusting God during impossible circumstances, about God being an anchor in the storm, about hope.

Then came the pandemic. And immediately thereafter, every time Michael checked on that exhibit, he noticed that Americans were no longer searching from a place of strength but rather a place of desperation. They now needed assurance too. They now needed hope. Verses such as John 16:33, where Jesus said, "I have told you these things, so that in me you may have peace. In this world you will have trouble. But take heart! I have overcome the world," and 2 Corinthians 4:17, which says, "For our light and momentary troubles are achieving for us an eternal glory that far outweighs them all."

Candidly, for the past twelve months, Michael and I would

number ourselves among those people begging God for a little encouragement that everything is going to be okay somehow. For reasons having little to do with the actual pandemic, we, too, have needed some hope.

Beautiful Boy

As I write this, it was two years ago, almost to the day, that Michael and I brought home our baby boy, Ezra. And it was one year, almost to the day, that we had to let him go. Relinquishing any child you thought would be part of your family forever is an all-but-impossible ask, but Ezra made the occasion infinitely more difficult by being his adorable, easygoing self. I look back at photos from the year we had him under our roof and shake my head in awe over how God could have created such a perfect being. Those almond-shaped eyes that crinkled in the corners; his swoon-worthy comma-shaped eyebrows; his gorgeous mess of curly hair; that near-toothless wry grin; those pillowy cheeks; his sweet "uhn, uhn, uhhhhn!" that meant a million different things, depending on the situation he was trying desperately to control; his distinctive way of clapping his hands, holding one palm flat to the sky and slapping the other palm against it; his backward crawl that always left Michael, Zion, and me in stitches. My Ezra was a joy!

We're coming up on the Christmas holiday here in North America as I write this, and the fact that we lost that boy at this particular time of year feels like a truckload of salt in a raw, open wound. I was trying to get ready for church yesterday but ended up scrolling through the last year of pictures, wondering silently if this gaping hole in my heart would ever be filled again.

It's okay. I'll be okay, eventually. Ultimately, I know these things to be true. But for now, while things are feeling anniversary-ish and terrible and not very Christmasy at all, I'll just let myself sit here in the grief and pain.

Would the agony be lighter if our adoption efforts this past year had panned out and we had a baby to show for that work? I don't know. Honestly, I don't. All I know is that I miss Ezra—and that I still need hope.

An Unwelcome Farewell

As with all stories that touch on the adoption or potential adoption of a child, the backstory on how Ezra came to be in our lives is a complicated one. It should never have happened this way, truth be told, with our trying to move forward with the adoption process with him and then, after twelve straight months of being in limbo and waiting for finalization, having to give him up. But this is where we, too, were affected by the pandemic and by its effect on the court system nationwide. Things slowed to a crawl, cases were backlogged, judges were unavailable, and families dealing with all sorts of needs and problems were forced to just kind of hang tight. There was no communication, nothing to forewarn us that storm clouds were gathering. It's just that things were being pushed forward within the judicial system—albeit at a snail's pace—that would totally upend our lives.

When Ezra's court date to review his case finally rolled around and the decision was made to dismiss our adoption case altogether, Michael and I left the courthouse and drove home in silence. All the reframing in the world couldn't help us now. Ezra would be leaving our family. We'd already put Ezra down for a nap when we got a shocking follow-up call from our social worker informing us of the transfer plan. Weeks prior, our lawyer had said that in the event we had to turn over custody of Ezra, we would have some time with him before handing him off. Christmas was eight days from the trial, and our lawyer had said in cases like ours, we'd have a week, maybe two.

That day on the phone, we were told we had just under three hours. We were ordered to arrive at a lawyer's office by 6:00 p.m. and hand Ezra over.

Today.

Not one or two weeks from now, but today.

"What?" I yelled into the phone to our social worker.

"I know . . ." she replied. I could tell she, too, was stunned. Her voice quavered as if she might cry.

I ended the call and looked at my watch. It was ten after three in the afternoon. "We have just over two hours," I said to Michael. "Let's get the kids up now."

We had consulted with family friends who are in the counseling profession as to whether we should tell Zion ahead of time that there was a possibility Ezra could leave our home. After wrestling with different scenarios, we had agreed that we needn't tell Zion what was going on until she absolutely needed to know. We didn't want to worry a three-year-old's heart unnecessarily, and from everything our lawyer had told us, it was very likely Ezra could remain with us forever. For all of Michael's and my obsessive worst-case-scenario planning over the years, somehow neither of us had prepped for this. We had to tell Zion now.

In a flash, as I headed upstairs for Zion's room, the injustices we'd suffered flew through my mind, a ticker tape of tragedy that just wouldn't stop.

This was this judge's first ruling on an adoption case. I mean, he'd been a family court judge for only two weeks!

We've had this child for a full year, and the ruling was to dismiss the adoption as though it had never occurred? It did occur! We were there! We've been there for Ezra for twelve solid months!

We were told we'd have ten to fourteen days. This was not ten to fourteen days.

We've sacrificed to pay thousands in adoption and legal fees to ensure Ezra's case was fairly heard. And now it is also going to cost us this deeply painful experience.

I reached Zion's bedside and placed my cheek beside hers. "Zi," I whispered. "Zi, Daddy and I are waking you up early today. We want to play with you and brother."

Zion's eyes opened, but it took her a minute to emerge from her discombobulated dreamland. "Mommy?" she said.

"Yes, baby girl. Mommy's here. We're going to have a short nap today so that you and Ezra and Daddy and I can have some playtime together."

Michael was there now too, and we walked downstairs together and sat on the living room floor as we tried to gently explain that her brother was going to have to go away. She rubbed her eyes and knitted her eyebrows together, trying to grasp what our heavy words meant.

Michael went to get Ezra up from his nap, and then we would all meet in the playroom downstairs to have our final family time together. Michael was always the one to get Ezra up from his nap, and as he would walk down the stairs, he'd made a habit of praying over Ezra, of thanking God for letting him be Ezra's dad and begging God to let him stay. During this slow walk down the stairs today, though, Michael recognized that it was time for the way he prayed for Ezra to change. He wasn't going to stay. The Lord's will was not as we had wished.

I sometimes wonder what God thought of all those prayers, knowing what was to come as he did.

The four of us convened in the quiet of the playroom and hung out for a while, determined to keep things as normal and sweet as they always were. Then Michael and I looked at each other, simultaneously struck by the same thought. We would go to the homes of each of our parents and let them have time with Ezra before our final goodbye. Within a few texts, all my family was set to meet at my sister Danielle's house, and Michael's brother and his wife would meet up with his mom at her house. They had loved him, too, and embraced him as part of our family. They each got to see him for about fifteen minutes to say goodbye.

No shortage of squishes and kisses and prayers were offered at those two brief stops, while Michael and I tried to shield Zion from the buckets of tears being shed. We then left her with Michael's mom and made the drive to drop Ezra off.

I remember so little about that twenty-minute trip—just that the radio wasn't on, that Michael and I weren't saying anything, and that Michael and I were facing one way and Ezra, all tucked into his comfy car seat, was facing another, all of which should have been a signal to me of what was to come.

"Take good care of him," I said as I handed over that precious boy.

We walked back to the car before the dam burst and we began to weep. We were less than one hundred feet from Ezra. He was just on the other side of that office door where we left him. Yet we couldn't see him, and we would never see him again. We held each other and allowed ourselves to cry before heading back to face, once again, the reality of being a family of three that longed to be a family of four.

Would Ezra's new caregiver know that when Ezra was upset

and crying, he liked his head to be scratched instead of his back? That he liked to be held close and bounced when he was tired? That he loved music and being in the sun when he was upset? Regarding that and a thousand other questions, devastatingly we'd never find out.

These days, even with the pain still present, I'm able to say with all confidence that the plan for Ezra's life was not just allowed by God but was ordained by him. God himself had orchestrated those events.

Now I'm better able to understand that my role in the whole ordeal was to believe that God's plan was the right plan. To be thankful to God that he'd trusted us to care for Ezra during those critical first twelve months of his life. And, as Jochebed did with Moses sixteen centuries prior, to release Ezra on the unknowable waters of life, hopeful that goodness and mercy indeed would follow him all the days of his life.

A Theology of Hope

A curious thing about my personality is that I'm not really one to feel my feelings much. I used to think everyone processed life on a cerebral level and nothing else—that is, until I met people who experienced strange things such as, you know, emotions, and I realized that maybe I was odd.

I don't know if we'd call it good news or bad news that I married someone just like me, but it's news, I guess, in the sense that for a couple who has gone through so much trauma, we don't really experience it as such. I've cried. I've raged. For sure, I've had moments of normal-people things. But in terms of how I encounter the ups and downs of everyday life, a "feeling" person I am not.

Here's where this tendency helps me: At the end of the day or week or season of terrible pain, I can generally "logic" my way back to what I know to be true, regardless of how I (would if I could?) feel. And what that logic reminds me, hour by hour, day by day, is that those of us who abide in Christ are headed for victory someday.

THOSE OF US WHO ABIDE IN CHRIST ARE HEADED FOR VICTORY SOMEDAY.

Last year, mere days after we'd lost Ezra, Michael and Zion and I headed to Walt Disney World for a trip that my parents had planned for us all months before. I remember thinking how absurd it felt to be packing to go to a vacation theme park when my heart was breaking into a million sharp shards. *Maybe the getaway will be good for us*, I thought. Maybe we just needed some sunshine, some warmth, some funnel cake, some Minnie Mouse ears. Pain narrows our focus, doesn't it? Maybe Disney would expand it some.

Listen, I'm a raving fan of Disney theme parks and all, but you know as well as I do that that trip did nothing but temporarily distract me from the truckload of trauma that was waiting for me once I got home. Had I simply reread a little from Revelation 21 before boarding our flight, I could have saved us a ton of money and a week's worth of time if we had wanted to.

> Then I saw "a new heaven and a new earth," for the first heaven and the first earth had passed away, and there was no longer any sea. I saw the Holy City, the new Jerusalem, coming down out of heaven from God, prepared as a bride beautifully dressed for her husband. And I heard a loud voice from the throne saying, "Look! God's dwelling place is now among the

> people, and he will dwell with them. They will be his people, and God himself will be with them and be their God. 'He will wipe every tear from their eyes. There will be no more death' or mourning or crying or pain, for the old order of things has passed away." (vv. 1–5)

Hope is found in the new heaven and new earth, in our eternal dwelling with God. And guess who made that togetherness possible? The resurrected Jesus Christ.

As much as I hated to admit it, my hope was not going to be found in having Ezra returned to us, despite how deeply I wanted that to occur. It was going to be found only in my Lord and Savior, Jesus, in his death and burial and rising from the grave. "Whatever catastrophe may end this world is merely a tool in God's hand to build the new heavens and the new earth," Ligon Duncan wrote. "Whatever you fear may cause God's promises to fail will likely be the very thing he uses to fulfill them."[1]

As I sat with the expansive vision of all that God was doing to bring about his new heaven, his new earth, I considered for the first time that the only way I could deal with the loss of Ezra was by knowing that I'd have more of God.

Author Lysa TerKeurst once wrote that when suffering comes, hope means "we have a place to look."[2] We have a place to look. We have a place to stay. We have a place to lay our heads and find comfort for our distress.

That Anchor in the Storm

Weeks after Disney, I did eventually get to spend some time with the words of Revelation 21, refreshing myself on the "new thing" that God said he was doing. I couldn't help but think of the prophet Isaiah's words in Isaiah 43:18–21, where, speaking on behalf of God, he said,

> Forget the former things; do not dwell on the past. See, I am doing a new thing! Now it springs up; do you not perceive it? I am making a way in the wilderness and streams in the wasteland. The wild animals honor me, the jackals, and the owls, because I provide water in the wilderness and streams in the wasteland, to give drink to my people, my chosen, the people I formed for myself that they may proclaim my praise.

As it related to my relationship with sweet Ezra, I would never truly forget the "former things," but something about that promise of newness resonated with me. Deep inside my soul, I longed for that brand-new thing.

One of my personal heroes has always been the inimitable English writer, philanthropist, playwright, and activist Hannah More, who lived in London from the mid-eighteenth to mid-nineteenth centuries. I read one time that halfway through her life, although she would continue her work and service among those who were destitute—sort of a Mother Teresa of her time—she decided to relocate her residence from the harried and bustling city center to a quiet plot of land in rural Britain, where she could keep animals and a garden plot. The way she described her motivation for the move was by saying that she "intended to escape from the world gradually," a phrase that seems applicable to me now. To hold fast to divinely enabled hope while still longing to hold on to the people and experiences and things in this temporal existence is also a way to escape the world gradually, I suppose. We know a new thing, a better thing, is coming.

WE KNOW A NEW THING, A BETTER THING, IS COMING.

Still, over the past year I have been practicing that turn, that "throwing of my focus forward,"[3] as author Orlando Saer calls it, that conscious clinging to the hope of God. Were the Bible Now exhibit to broadcast my most-searched verses of late, in addition to Revelation 21, it would say that I've been camped out on verses such as Psalm 147:11, which says, "The LORD delights in those who fear him, who put their hope in his unfailing love." And on Proverbs 23:18: "There is surely a future hope for you, and your hope will not be cut off." And on Romans 15:13: "May the God of hope fill you with all joy and peace as you trust in him, so that you may overflow with hope by the power of the Holy Spirit." And on 1 Timothy 4:10: "That is why we labor and strive, because we have put our hope in the living God, who is the Savior of all people, and especially of those who believe." And on the potent appeal in Romans 12:12 to "be joyful in hope, patient in affliction, faithful in prayer."

Dr. Tony Evans once wrote that when we have a "low view of God in crisis," it means that the crisis can own us. But when we have a "high view of God," the crisis no longer has the last word.[4] And while I can't put my finger on exactly when the thought occurred to me, over the first weeks and months when Ezra was gone but I was still in touch with his birth mom, I realized that God was carving out a new capacity in my heart for compassion and sympathy and advocacy for teenage moms, single moms, and moms in crisis of all sorts. For years I've worked in a leadership capacity for a pro-life collaborative network whose aim is to uphold the value of human dignity by protecting babies in the womb and caring well for women and families facing unplanned pregnancies. Coming to know Ezra's mom through our weekly communications helped me better understand the distinct challenges she'd been up against in bringing Ezra into the world.

His mom—I'll call her Jenny—had been an orphan herself, having lost her mother when she was just a seven-month-old baby. With no father in the picture and no knowledge of either set of grandparents, Jenny had been raised by her great-grandmother. But then when she was only fifteen years old, Jenny lost that lone relative. For the next twelve months, she stayed with that great-grandmother's third husband, who had just gotten out of prison, but by the time she turned sixteen she decided to move out on her own.

Her junior year, Jenny got pregnant with Ezra. Imagine: you've just turned seventeen years old, you're living on your own and flipping burgers at McDonald's after school, you're trying to keep up with your studies, and you're pregnant and trying to figure out what to do, with relatively no support.

I love that Jenny gave life to her child. Against so many odds, she brought that baby into the world.

Now, whenever I hear about a woman with an unplanned pregnancy who is considering abortion, I reflexively think of Jenny. I think about all the possible pain points this woman could be facing, and now I know just how deep that pain can run, based on all that Jenny faced. The truth is that almost no one wants to get an abortion. Most women have abortions because they believe they have no other choice. The pain in their lives is so ridiculously sky-high that they decide the awfulness of the abortion will still be a better solution than dealing with the awfulness of trying to juggle everything they've got going on while also becoming a mom.

I can now empathize more with their plight; I understand as I'd never understood before. And I have Ezra—and his mom—to thank for that.

I don't think we can always find purpose in the pain we face—I hope you hear me on that. While I've made progress in my acceptance of God's plans for our family and for Ezra these past two years, it's not like I've found a way to tie it up with a big red bow. Not at all. Some days are brutal still. But what I will say is that I've found a way to remember that God is God, and I am not. I've found a way to remind my heart of what my head has believed all along: that he is all-knowing. That he is committed to my good. That he loves Ezra more than I could ever dream of loving him—and I sure loved that little boy. I love that little boy still.

In moments when my heart starts to ache for Ezra, I remember that God is worthy of attaching every bit of hope to him because he alone is where hope is found.

On Wishing the Phone Hadn't Rung

After the dust had settled a little following the trial, Michael and I wanted to be intentional about providing space and resources for Zion to make sure she felt supported in processing the loss of her brother. So we researched and scheduled a few counseling sessions for Zion with a child specialist we knew. The counselor was familiar with our situation and had earlier helped us preemptively plan out how to explain Ezra's departure should that become our reality. The counselor explained that communicating Ezra's departure to Zion, a three-year-old at the time, would best be done by putting words to several simple scenes with her.

When that fateful day came that we said goodbye to Ezra, we walked through our rehearsed explanation, reminding Zion that we'd been such a happy threesome, when it was just Mommy and Daddy and her. Then we'd said that one day the phone rang, and Mommy and Daddy learned that they got to adopt another child, this time a son. We'd reminded her that we'd been such a happy foursome after that: Mommy, Daddy, Zion, and Ezra—one big, beloved family. But then the phone rang again and it was a sad phone call, and we'd learned that Ezra was going to be part of another family now, that we were going to go back to being a threesome—Mommy and Daddy and Zion—and that one day, despite how sad we felt about that right now, we'd be better. We'd be happy again.

Unbeknownst to us, that counselor had asked her husband, a graphic designer, to lay out those scenes in something of a flip-book that Zion could keep with her and look at to remind herself that someday things would be okay, that someday she'd feel happy again, and that the three of us—Zion, Michael, and I—would always stay together.

Tears sprang to my eyes as I took in the simple images: On page one, a very handsome bald man with a red beard standing next to a snow-white woman with red hair, both holding hands with a tiny Asian girl. Smiles all around. On pages two and three, an iPhone ringing . . . a beautiful Black baby . . . more smiles to come. On page four, another ringing phone, and then page five, the three of us, sad. Still today, Zion always stops on page five, not quite ready to move to the end. "I wish we didn't get that bad call," she says, her way of sitting with her pain for a beat. "I really wish that, Mommy."

"I wish that too," I always tell my girl.

I really wish that too.

A CHANCE TO COLLECT YOUR THOUGHTS

Sit with your thoughts before God for a few minutes, paying attention to how you're feeling as you read each question to yourself. Take as much time as you need before moving on in the book.

The Complete Relief We Seek

1. What comfort have you found in surrendering to the idea that "God's plan is the right plan"? What role does faith play in assuming this type of posture?
2. What comfort have you found in accepting that "God is God, and we are not"?
3. What comfort have you found in looking ahead to the new heaven and new earth we will one day inhabit (Revelation 21:1)?

CHAPTER 9

PEACE

When All Is Well

Go in peace.

—JESUS

MICHAEL

The night before Zion's cancer surgery, some of our closest friends reached out and asked if they could come to the hospital to pray over us and our daughter. One of the couples that showed up serves in North Africa as missionaries. They happened to be in town just before we headed for China to pick up Zion earlier that year in August 2019, so they stayed with us and helped paint the nursery as they listened to us dream about what it would be like to become parents. They happened to be back in town now—in October, which meant they could finally meet Zion in person. It was special to have these friends, who now lived halfway across the world, back with us at this pivotal moment. Four other couples who had been best friends with us for years—some of them since our middle school days—joined us as well. Lauren and I would have a soft place to land. We had a steady and present group of friends at the ready to encourage us and to keep reminding us that we could trust God despite the pain.

Thankfully, Zion did very well in surgery, and within a few weeks she was set to begin chemotherapy treatments. Which brings me to the scene I'll replay. Lauren and I were in the hospital room with Zion when a team of nurses and aides came in to give us an update and let us know Zion would need a peripherally inserted central catheter (PICC) line. The line didn't have to run through her chest, they informed us, but through her arm. It was a better scenario for our daughter, they said, as it was less invasive. It would require a minor procedure, though, to get the PICC line inserted and connected to a main artery so that they could use this access line for the sedation, lab draws, and, later, the chemo.

That minor procedure didn't go quite as planned.

Zion had been given some light anesthesia as the doctor and nurses worked to get the PICC line inserted into the proper place up her arm and near her heart. After a few attempts, they were unsuccessful. Even worse, the line had coiled inside Zion's vein.

"We've never seen this before," the nurse said. If they pulled out the line, it could do damage to the vein. If they left it in, that coil could pinch, restricting the flow of medicine into little Zion's body. They needed to send her to a different floor and into a surgery room with more sophisticated equipment to fix what had happened.

It was this incident that put my wife and me over the edge. Lauren broke down, which prompted our kind pediatric oncologist to reach for a tissue and comfort her as much as he could.

Unsettled, we headed to the surgery center, hopeful that the doctor could fix the PICC line.

Made Good

Just before Jesus faced his crucifixion, he gathered his disciples in the upper room to share a final meal together. He washed their feet. He issued a reminder to them to love God and love his people. He told the disciples that once he was gone, a Helper, the Holy Spirit, would come to them to guide them in all truth. And then, because Jesus knew they would feel fearful navigating life without him, maybe even abandoned like a child left on an orphanage's steps, he told the disciples, "Peace I leave with you; my peace I give you. I do not give to you as the world gives. Do not let your hearts be troubled and do not be afraid" (John 14:27).

Peace. *Shalom*—literally "made good," "fully restored," "set at one again"—the sense is that whatever was missing has been returned, that whatever was lacking has been replaced, whatever was fractured has been brought back together again.

The day after that PICC line incident, as we arrived for Zion's first chemo drip, we heard cheerful whoops and singing as we stepped out of the elevator onto the cancer floor. It was the first Wednesday of December, and while we were rookies with respect to the annual rhythms of the place, the first Wednesday of December is evidently when the moms of the kids who were being treated for cancer banded together to throw an over-the-top Christmas party for the unit. It wasn't until I was faced with an influx of holiday cheer that I realized how withdrawn I'd been. In fact, I hadn't even realized that the holiday was upon us. For weeks I'd been guarded, fractured, anticipating more setbacks in life—more frustrations, more obstacles, more pain. But now the environment forced me to choose: Would I continue in that closed-off spirit or would I accept the invitation to change?

I looked down at Zion, whose hand I was holding, and saw her fix her gaze on a massive, beautifully decorated Christmas tree that stood proudly in the center of the waiting room, and then it occurred to me that my daughter had never seen a Christmas tree. She'd been in a Chinese orphanage her first year and a half of life and then had come to us in the summertime. Zion had never experienced Christmas, and the last thing I was going to do was lead her through it as a Scrooge. There in the oncology wing of the ninth floor east in the Oklahoma Children's Hospital, I chose a posture that matched the season; I chose the posture of peace.

Peace like the theme of the second advent candle our church had lit the Sunday prior.

Or maybe peace chose me.

The Pursuing God

Throughout Scripture we get these pictures of God searching for us, looking for us, coming to us, hoping we'll respond. I think of 2 Chronicles 16:9, which says, "For the eyes of the LORD range throughout the earth to strengthen those whose hearts are fully committed to him. You have done a foolish thing, and from now on you will be at war." And of Revelation 3:20, where Jesus said, "Here I am! I stand at the door and knock. If anyone hears my voice and opens the door, I will come in and eat with that person, and they with me."

And in the parable of the lost sheep in Luke 15 we learn of God's pursuit of us in this way.

> Suppose one of you has a hundred sheep and loses one of them. Doesn't he leave the ninety-nine in the open country and go after the lost sheep until he finds it? And when he finds it, he joyfully puts it on his shoulders and goes home. Then he calls his friends and neighbors together and says, "Rejoice with me; I have found my lost sheep." I tell you that in the same way there will be more rejoicing in heaven over one sinner who repents than over ninety-nine righteous persons who do not need to repent. (vv. 4–7)

And then there's the ultimate demonstration of pursuit: God sending his Son to earth in human form. "But when the set time had fully come," Galatians 4:4–5 says, "God sent his Son, born of a woman, born under the law, to redeem those under the law, that we might receive adoption to sonship."

God is pursuing us, coming toward us, positioning himself within reach through the sacrifice of his Son. And if only we'll abandon all our other pursuits—of control, of power, of independence, of freedom on our limited terms—we'll find in his presence everything we could ever hope for: abundance, contentment, and, yes, peace. Peace when our time is crunched. Peace when our energy is sapped. Peace when our heart is broken. Peace for whatever we face.

Taking Control Versus Taking Heart

I've noticed a funny thing about how I tend to respond when problems come my way, which is at the center of why my wife and I wanted to write this book. When trouble comes, I want to control the situation. Lauren is similarly afflicted with the tendency to take control. When my dad told me that he and my mom were divorcing, I tried to take control by talking him into reversing course. When years went by with nothing happening on the adoption front, I tried to take control by strategizing and scheming and bartering with God. When Zion was diagnosed with cancer seven weeks after we'd brought her home, I tried to take control by obsessing over every detail, evaluating the situation from every conceivable side. When Ezra was slipping from our grip and we were faced with having to give him up, I strategized compulsively, looking for any way of keeping him before the judge declared that handing Ezra over was all I could do.

We do these things, don't we? When things don't go our way,

our reflexive reaction is to grasp for control, to organize and systematize and negotiate and strategize and plot and plan and make bold declarations of what we'll do if things don't get turned around fast.

In short, we talk a good game, even as our words are impotent fluff.

At some point in our lives, we all come to a place when we realize that we are not in control; God is. But we still have a hard time acknowledging the fact that control over our lives is not ours to be had. But here's why that's a very good thing: the one who does have control is very good at controlling things, and under his purview we can live at ease.

Think of it: How would you like to be tasked with controlling the universe, with ensuring that whatever you caused or allowed to happen you could then weave together for ultimate good? If you're like me, you think all your troubles would fade in a jiffy if you could just have control for a sec. If only you could orchestrate life to run on your terms, toward your ends, with your well-being in mind, then life would be a joyous experience. Life would be a ball.

But would it?

A quick jaunt through history ought to prove to you and me both that when humankind gets their hands on things, those things tend to devolve—fast. "Don't touch that tree." We touched the tree. "Don't harm your brother." We killed our brother. "Don't worship other gods." We worshiped other gods. Time and again when we encountered divinely placed Wet Paint signs, we just couldn't help ourselves; we tiptoed over and touched.

Remember in the Old Testament when the Israelites begged God for a king? The prophet Samuel, the same one who was raised in the temple and who heard God's voice as a young boy, was serving as a judge over the nation of Israel and in his old age decided to appoint his sons as judges too. But those sons lacked integrity and, according to 1 Samuel 8:3, "turned aside after dishonest gain" by taking bribes and perverting justice.

Well, the elders of the nation grew weary of these miscreants' behavior and came to Samuel, saying, "You are old, and your sons do not follow your ways; now appoint a king to lead us, such as all the other nations have" (v. 5).

This is so like us, isn't it? We're like petulant children whining, "We want what theeeeyyy have."

Samuel knew this was a bad idea, but he conferred with God anyway. He prayed for wisdom, and here is what happened next:

> And the LORD told him: "Listen to all that the people are saying to you; it is not you they have rejected, but they have rejected me as their king. As they have done from the day I brought them up out of Egypt until this day, forsaking me and serving other gods, so they are doing to you. Now listen to them; but warn them solemnly and let them know what the king who will reign over them will claim as his rights." (vv. 7–9)

Samuel did as he was told. He went back to the people and told them that God was going to grant them a king but that their king wouldn't be all that they hoped for. No, instead that king would take their sons and appoint them to his chariots to be his horsemen. That king would appoint many commanders for his armies and make the people plow his ground and reap his harvest for him. That king would take their daughters and make them work long hours as his cooks and bakers. That king would rob them of their best fields and vineyards, taking a tenth of their grain and grapes for himself, free of charge (vv. 11–17). "When that day comes," Samuel concluded his warning, "you will cry out for relief from the king you have chosen, but the LORD will not answer you in that day" (v. 18).

In response, guess what the Israelites said to Samuel? In effect, "Eh. We're sure we'll be fine."

You and I do the same dumb thing still today. We're just *sure* that we can do better than God's kingship, that we can be in better control than he. We're just *sure* that we'll be okay. And so, we charge ahead, living just like everyone else we see, putting anything and everything but God on the throne of our hearts and lives. We put our careers and our paychecks there. We put "expert" opinions there. We put habits and addictions there. We put good intentions there. We put self-help there. We put the noblest of things there: our spouse, our kids, our ministry, our church. The church is a God thing, right?

And just like the Israelites saw, when their demands for a king led to a generations-long string of mostly awful, evil leaders who only brought strife to the nation they led, we can't help but notice that our self-focused, solution-seeking efforts only leave us more anxious and scattered in the end. What we hoped would cause our lives to feel as though things have been "made good" again just ushers in more chaos as we wonder what in the world we've done.

All the while, God tries to get our attention: *If you'll let me take my rightful place in your life, things will work much better for you. Taking control was never the plan for you. The plan was for you to take heart in me, to let me be your source for peace.*

Choosing Peace Today and Always

If you are tangled up in knots right now, wondering how to get out of the confusion and chaos that have wound their way around your life, I have good news for you. The same God who has been pursuing his people since the beginning of time is waiting, at hand, for you now. He comes in peace. He is formed of peace. He longs to usher peace into your life. But this isn't something he will force on you. This is something you must choose. Let's look at how to choose peace today, with all its challenges, with all its struggles, with all its strife.

In Psalm 139:23–24, David prayed what is perhaps the boldest prayer in all of Scripture: "Search me, God, and know my heart; test me and know my anxious thoughts. See if there is any offensive way in me, and lead me in the way everlasting."

This is a prayer of examination, of scrutiny, of assessment. Here, David invited God to look not just at David's actions—the stuff on the outside—but at his heart and mind, the innermost part of himself. David proved with this invitation that he was not trying to see how much sin he could get away with and still call himself a follower of God. No, he was trying to see how obedient he could be while still living as a fallen man.

If you're having trouble accessing peace amid life's sometimes stormy seas, ask God to search you and know your heart, to try you and know your thoughts. Invite him to probe the innermost part of you to see what might be askew. In my own life, whenever I'm bringing things like anxiety and chaos and disorder and confusion to a situation instead of sweet, calm, life-giving peace, ten times out of ten, I'm neglecting in that moment to believe that God is who he says he is and that he is doing what he said he would do. So, I ask, *Father, what am I not believing about you? In your presence is peace, so what unbelief is leading me away from the peace to be found here with you?*

We're not going to get it right 100 percent of the time. Even the most peaceful people I know flub from time to time. Welcome to the human condition, where not even one of us lives a perfect life. Here's what matters: When you mess up, make things right. Claim God's forgiveness. Make amends. Do better next time.

Ask God to lead you out of that momentary unbelief and into the "everlasting way," as David called it. And move forward in . . . any guesses?

Move forward in perfect peace.

We need this exhortation today, wouldn't you agree? If there is one thing sorely lacking in our culture today, it is the God-given spirit of peace. And yet in Jesus, it's here, at hand. We don't have to work for it, fight for it, or beg for it. We simply have to let it be operational in our lives.

If peace seems elusive, you may not need a complete overhaul of your faith; you may just need a time-out. The recovery movement's HALT acronym is as well known as it is for a reason: if you suspect you might be hungry, angry, lonely, or tired, you've found the source of your distress. To reconnect with peace, consider addressing those more fundamental needs first. Once your body is tended to, your heart will have an easier time remembering what is true: that God is near, that God is peace, and that peace is yours.

Peace in the Pain

I've often thought about what a gift it is that Jesus endured every ounce of temptation and struggle that you and I endure, even as he did not sin. I find it wildly comforting that Jesus can relate to what I'm going through. Jesus knows what it is like to have strained family relationships like me. Jesus knows the pain of losing a loved one like me. Jesus knows the betrayal of a close friend like me. He gets us. Which is why I believe he promised us peace. It's worth pausing here to confirm in your heart and mine that we were never promised a pain-free existence. We just weren't. I know we think it would make things a whole lot easier if salvation came with such a guarantee, but that isn't how this life works.

God doesn't stand back as we struggle and try to convince us the pain doesn't exist. It does exist. Of course it exists. To think otherwise would be delusion. But in his very presence, what God declares over us is that our pain doesn't exist in a vacuum. There is a context in which that pain does not get to win. And by his power, accompanied by prevailing peace, God will walk us from here to there in safety, holding our hand each step of the way.

Who Might You Become?

Sometimes when I'm enjoying a few unhurried moments with God, my thoughts drift to gratitude—specifically, to how grateful I am that I don't have to try to do life without him. Have you ever thought—really thought—about who you would be apart from the empowerment of God by his Spirit? And about who you would become?

I was talking with a colleague last week about this topic, and I said in all honesty, "Without the love and hope and peace of God flowing through me, I think I'd quickly become a bitter old man."

Now, I recognize that by everyone's standard except maybe that of a teenager, I'm not old. But like me, you've probably met people along the way who seemed far older than they were. Somewhere along the way, the stresses of life aged them, making them angry, cynical, and hard. It's no exaggeration for me to say that that's who I would be apart from God. I dislike pain, remember? Also, I have a huge justice streak. Even small things get to me, like drivers who do not respect merge signs on the highway and cut in front of dozens of cars waiting patiently to endure the "lane closed" traffic. You tell me: How does that type of person make it in life apart from God's perspective and peace? He doesn't. He gets colder as he gets older and most likely finishes life all alone.

I don't know who you would become, apart from God's presence, apart from the fruit of his Spirit being reflected in your life, but I imagine that you do. You know what your points of vulnerability are. You know where you would struggle and fail. You know the proclivities you'd have the most trouble overcoming. You know exactly what you're capable of apart from God. I know what I'm capable of too.

Here's what that knowledge can do in your heart and in mine: it can create in us a real sense of urgency to reestablish God as the one in control.

You will not find peace by insisting on stirring things up. Based on the beautiful truth noted in Psalm 29:11—"The Lord gives strength to his people; the Lord blesses his people with peace"—you will find peace by surrendering to God.

A CHANCE TO COLLECT YOUR THOUGHTS

Sit with your thoughts before God for a few minutes, paying attention to how you're feeling as you read each question to yourself. Take as much time as you need before moving on in the book.

Serenity Within Despite Troubles Without

1. What does it mean to you to know that if you have accepted Jesus as Lord, then you are an adopted child of God?
2. How do you respond to this idea?

> God is pursuing us, coming toward us, positioning himself within reach through the sacrifice of his Son. And if only we'll abandon all our other pursuits—of control, of power, of independence, of freedom on our limited terms—we'll find in his presence everything we could ever hope for: abundance, contentment, and, yes, peace. Peace when our time is crunched. Peace when our energy is sapped. Peace when our heart is broken. Peace for whatever we face.

3. Have you ever prayed the words of Psalm 139:23–24, which asks God to search you and know your heart, to test you and know your anxious thoughts? Given your life circumstances during this season, what do you think such an assessment would yield?

CHAPTER 10

PERSPECTIVE

An Eye Toward the Eternal

Loss can give us clarity about some things. It strips us of pretense, vanity, or waste. It gives a season of rare simplicity, freedom, and equilibrium.

—JERRY SITTSER

LAUREN

A memory comes to mind.

It's a typical Wednesday morning in November 2019, and I'm eager to be getting back to work after taking some maternity leave since the adoption of our first child—our daughter, Zion. Before I head to the office, I need to take Zion to have a scheduled X-ray as part of a routine checkup. There have been signs that she may have a minor issue that will require surgery on her spine, and the doctors want to check things out. Michael and I will drop by the hospital together, wait while the smart people take the necessary X-rays, and head into our respective plans.

Results from those images will be ready in a few hours, we are told. We'll be called when the doctor knows more.

I work for a family business that my grandfather founded, and we have monthly business meetings that are preceded by a lunch for family members who are able to attend. I'm excited that Michael and Zion will be joining me at the office for this family lunch before I need to slip away. Although Zion is already twenty months old, she has been in our family for only seven weeks' time and is still getting to know some of our extended family. Each of these interactions goes a long way in helping her feel at home.

It's a joy to have Zion—my daughter . . . how sweet that thought is to me—around my work environment, connecting with family, and perhaps because I am so engrossed with her, I don't notice a string of missed calls. As we finish eating and I am chatting with my aunt, I see in my peripheral vision that Michael has picked up Zion and is hurriedly packing her things.

Before I can shoot him a look that asks what the rush is about, he is crossing the space between us in three strides and telling me we need to go. "I'm taking Zion and loading the car," he says, not even catching my eye. "We'll wait for you out front."

Not sharing my husband's sense of urgency, I end the conversation I'm having and make my way to the parking lot.

"I just heard back from the pediatrician," Michael tells me as I climb into the front seat and buckle my belt. "She couldn't reach you, so she called me. She said that we need to come to her office right away."

I don't know what is up, but I know it can't be good. Doctors don't request urgent meetings to discuss inconsequential things.

"While we were looking at Zion's spine," the doctor is saying, now that we've entered her office and taken a seat, "we found a tumor on her liver. A large tumor, I'm afraid . . ."

As she continues to speak, I lose cognition. Her words sound all jumbled to me.

"It could be cancer," she says.

"We need to act," she says.

"We need Zion in the ER immediately," she says.

And so, we do as we are told.

We leave the pediatrician's office and drive to the Oklahoma Children's Hospital emergency room.

Three hours prior to that conversation, my biggest concern had centered on getting back to my career and sorting out how to be the working mom I wanted to be. My most significant stressors that morning had been finding a professional but functional outfit and nailing down a childcare solution for the coming week. Now my daughter's life is on the line. In an instant, my perspective has switched.

Earthly Versus Heavenly Perspective

Life is full of these switches, isn't it? We're moving through a typical day, when *bam*—everything shifts. For you, the switch might be due to the sudden loss of a job, your spouse's decision to file for divorce, the death of a loved one, a medical diagnosis, or some other crisis that in an instant can capture your attention and rattle your world. Whatever the catalyst, it changes your perspective. It changes your outlook on life.

Those defining moments in life sometimes provide a slight and momentary perspective shift. Other times, as was the case with Zion's cancer, they shape our day-to-day lives for weeks and linger forever in their effect. The perspective shift after Zion's cancer diagnosis was one of clarity; things like my outfit and even my career no longer mattered. My child's life was hanging in the balance, and that reality provided great clarity about the things that are important in life.

These shifts can be deeply unsettling. Your conscious and subconscious assumptions about life and the world are turned upside down, leaving you to wonder what is safe to assume. It is shaking a layer of your foundation, which leaves you to inspect everything that was sitting on your foundational beliefs. When Michael and I finally became parents, I didn't have a category for walking my child through cancer. My subconscious assumption was that my child would grow to live an ever-increasingly healthy and vibrant life. When that assumption wasn't our reality, it caused a level of fear and worry for other parts of my life. What other assumptions did I have wrong? When was the other shoe going to drop in another aspect of life? When we place our hope in the things of this world, we will always find ourselves standing on shaky ground.

Perspective-shifting moments shape us. They shape our perspective of us in the world, and they shape our perspective of God. When we face these shifts, it is important to have a foundation to root us in truthful beliefs to guide us from one perspective into the next.

WHEN WE PLACE OUR HOPE IN THE THINGS OF THIS WORLD, WE WILL ALWAYS FIND OURSELVES STANDING ON SHAKY GROUND.

We can change our earthly perspective by shifting our eyes to an eternal perspective. Living with an eternal perspective means that we continue to fix our gaze on heaven. Having an eternal perspective is a steadying force in life. Living in our world with its pains, distractions, and challenges becomes more manageable when we have something that is constant. Taking the time to step outside of our earthly perspective, focus on God, and shift to an eternal perspective can be a game changer.

Seeing things in light of eternity doesn't mean that your earthly troubles go away. Looking toward heaven is never an excuse to diminish, downplay, or dismiss the pain we experience in our world. Having a trite "it will all eventually be okay in heaven" reply to pain is to deny the realities that we are living in this world here and now. Having an eye toward the eternal allows us to hold both the eternal and earthly in tension.

We live in the present, this broken world, with all its joys and pains. Assuming an eternal perspective means we accept the realities of the earthly one as well. But in doing so, we place our earthly realities in light of eternity.

Black Dot on the String

Perspective can be thought of as the way we think about life. Think about life in terms of its brevity. If eternity were a string of yarn wrapped all the way around the world, our life is briefer than a single dot placed anywhere along that yarn with a marker. We can live with just that black dot on the yarn as our understanding about life, or we can form our understanding of our black dot of life considering the rest of the miles of string. Viewing this life in light of eternity will ultimately bring more joy in the present.

How do we gain an eternal perspective? It starts with knowing Scripture. Michael and I are both passionate advocates for biblical literacy, which is why our first coauthorship was a book on that subject titled *Not What You Think: Why the Bible Might Be Nothing We Expected Yet Everything We Need*. We know the power of God's Word. We don't point people to Scripture for the sake of knowledge alone but for the sake of seeing their lives transformed as they strengthen their relationship and deepen their intimacy with God.

Our current culture, Christians included, has the lowest biblical literacy score ever recorded in the United States.[1] According to the American Bible Society's annual report, Bible engagement in America has been mostly trending downward since 2014. Every year it has maintained or gone down by one or two percentage points until 2021, when engagement increased by 2 percent. Most interestingly, in 2022 the percentage of Americans engaging in the Bible decreased by 10 percent. That means roughly twenty-six million Americans reduced or discontinued their engagement with the Bible in one year.[2]

Bible engagement matters. If people of faith don't know what the Bible says, they can't apply its truth as the foundation that shapes their ability to have an eternal perspective. A Christian's belief about God matters because with proper theology, our hearts can respond to God and our lives can be shaped by truth.[3]

There is a significant misunderstanding in our biblically illiterate culture about what the Bible teaches. Consider a recent report from Ligonier Ministries on the state of theology, which shows that in a broad survey of Americans, 67 percent of people agree that God accepts the worship of all religions, 53 percent say that Jesus was a great teacher but not God, 71 percent agree that "everyone is born innocent in the eyes of God," and only 51 percent agree that "the Bible is accurate in all it teaches."[4]

According to research from 2022, 63–69 percent of Americans identify as Christian.[5] While this means that nearly three out of four claim Christianity as their religious preference, that statistic represents a significant decline from the early 1990s, when 90 percent of Americans identified as Christian.[6]

The Top of Our Heart's Desire

For believers, having an eternal perspective comes from knowing what God says through his Word, the Bible; knowing what it teaches; and identifying how that is relevant for your life. When we are left with only an earthly perspective, then we live life trying to get all we can out of that tiny "black dot" of life, and the ups and downs in this short life are the only thing we have to affect how we feel. Living with only the black dot in mind will move our hearts to become more desperate for what we can hold on to and control in this world.

Whenever I think about the loss of the son I expected to adopt, if I am in the mindset of the black dot—meaning that I'm stuck in my earthly circumstances alone—the pain of the here and now is all I can see. I question God. I want to find happiness in this life, and having my son would have brought that. So why did God take him away?

On the flip side, when I'm able to step back to consider things in light of eternity, I view the situation differently, taking into account what God might be doing in my son's life that I'm not privy to because I don't see all that God sees. I can also see my pain in light of the hopeful future that is mine, knowing God will use it and work it together for his good. Developing my trust in God's providence is the key to finding peace in this life because we have more to live for than our earthly circumstances.

When Jesus spoke to his disciples about this earthly and heavenly divide, he said, "Do not store up for yourselves treasures on earth, where moths and vermin destroy, and where thieves break in and steal. But store up for yourselves treasures in heaven, where moths and vermin do not destroy, and where thieves do not break in and steal. For where your treasure is, there your heart will be also" (Matthew 6:19–21).

In verse 24 Jesus reminded us that ultimately "no one can serve two masters. Either you will hate the one and love the other, or you will be devoted to the one and despise the other. You cannot serve both God and money." The word "money" is translated from the Greek word for mammon, which can mean riches, money, possessions, or property.[7] The passage teaches us that we can't have our heart devoted to two masters simultaneously, for one master will always trump the other.

We may have many different things we love and serve to varying degrees in life, but only one can take top spot. If that sole master is earthly—money, power, pleasure . . . and also family, parenting, ministry work, serving others—then our hearts can't focus on our treasures being found in heaven. In claiming our best time and energy, they also take our hearts.

Whole-Heart Commitment

Our identity is not made for an earthly gaze. Saint Augustine touched on this concept long before I did when he wrote, "Our hearts are restless till they find rest in Thee."[8] As image bearers created in the image of God (Genesis 1:27), our heart's very identity and desire is for our Creator, not the created. We are made to reflect God so that we can bring his glory into our world. Doing anything less than that will never bring us fulfillment and purpose. God requires the whole heart, not our split attention. Focusing on earthly things as ultimate will bring anxiety; centering our hearts on the eternal will bring not only treasures in heaven someday but also greater peace and enjoyment in life here and now.

CENTERING OUR HEARTS ON THE ETERNAL WILL BRING NOT ONLY TREASURES IN HEAVEN BUT GREATER PEACE AND ENJOYMENT RIGHT NOW.

Maybe your life isn't centered on possessions and money but instead revolves around your relationships. Relationships aren't possessions and wealth, but even so, they can become idols when we value them more than we value

God. To value the relationships in our lives is good and right, but when those relationships, like possessions and money, take our gaze off God and onto worldly things, we are idolizing something we are not meant to worship.

Shifting our perspective from the temporal to the eternal is a daily practice that changes everything. Ultimately the perspective shift to the eternal is a shift that focuses on Jesus, our greatest treasure. In his letter to the Philippian church, the apostle Paul wrote, "What is more, I consider everything a loss because of the surpassing worth of knowing Christ Jesus my Lord, for whose sake I have lost all things. I consider them garbage, that I may gain Christ" (Philippians 3:8).

Paul certainly had his fair share of suffering and hardship. He had faced death, been beaten and shipwrecked, and endured a variety of other hardships in his life—yet he still maintained his posture of gratitude (2 Corinthians 11:23–27). Paul's hope was in Christ. He was looking to eternity and finding intimacy with God through the hardships and pain he faced in life.

Paul knew we would be wrestling between this earthly and heavenly perspective, admitting that "for we know that if the earthly tent we live in is destroyed, we have a building from God, an eternal house in heaven, not built by human hands. Meanwhile we groan, longing to be clothed instead with our heavenly dwelling." He then made this acknowledgment: "For we live by faith, not by sight" (2 Corinthians 5:1–2, 7). We must walk in what we believe about eternity, not by what we see on this earth.

I don't mean to sound trite or to imply that we should brush off the very real grief and hardships we will experience in this life. They are real and *ridiculously* tough. But while we acknowledge them, we must not forget to direct our hearts toward the hope we have in God and in his promises.

An Example Worth Following

I've watched both sets of my grandparents hold fast to hope throughout their lives and am grateful to be a beneficiary of their faith legacy. My grandpa, David Green, founded Hobby Lobby in his garage in 1970 with nothing more than a $600 loan. Today he still serves as CEO of the company, which has grown from one to more than one thousand stores,[9] and for as long as I've known him and worked with him, my grandfather has asked, "How can I be intentional with my work, my family, and my life, such that the legacy I leave goes beyond myself?"

The answer, it turns out, revolves around two practices: investing yourself in God's Word and investing in the souls of men and women. Investing in those things are ways we can pour in something that will matter for all eternity.

Hobby Lobby stores used to be open on Sundays—always one of the most profitable days of the week. But over time, Grandpa began to feel convicted that the stores should be closed so that employees had the opportunity to be with family and attend church if they desired. He decided to honor this conviction by closing all the stores in the state of Nebraska. Why did he start with Nebraska? At the time, there were only two stores there.

Once the media heard about these Nebraska Hobby Lobby stores being closed, they interviewed Grandpa about the decision, who shared that he was "trying it out in Nebraska." If it worked out, he said, he'd close the rest of the stores on Sundays too. A host of outlets ran with the article, and as Grandpa read his own words in black and white, his heart sank. He'd been planning to follow God's conviction only if it made financial sense to do so? This didn't sit right with him.

From that moment on, it was settled. On Sundays, *every* Hobby Lobby store would be closed, regardless of the decision's impact—financial or otherwise. By some estimates, Grandpa's decision would cost the company billions of dollars over the ensuing years, but I have to wonder: Did it wind up gaining them more than they lost, as customers saw a faithful follower of Jesus living fully devoted to God?

Good Times, Bad Times

When we live with an eternal perspective during good times, we will be more prone to adopting that mindset when challenges show up. Living in light of eternity can be a gift in the hard times because such a perspective reminds us that it won't always be this way. "For our light and momentary troubles are achieving for us an eternal glory that far outweighs them all," Paul wrote in 2 Corinthians 4:17.

For challenges that are significant, this perspective can remind us that during even the most challenging seasons, more glorious days lie ahead. With eternity in our future, we can see how Christ, "for the joy that was set before him endured the cross" (Hebrews 12:2 ESV). Christ faced the cross, with joy even, in part because he knew the promises of eternity.

Pain is a great revealer of our assumptions about God. What we assume to be true for God and his character will shape how we live and how we see our world. One particularly vivid moment when my assumptions about life were on display before me is when Zion was first diagnosed with cancer.

After our seven-year journey in the adoption process, when we finally adopted our daughter, only to receive a cancer diagnosis a month and a half later, I found myself thinking, *Haven't we done our time walking through pain related to becoming parents?*

The question itself betrayed my hidden belief, which was that God is good only insomuch as I define what "good" gets to look like.

As we discussed earlier, God is still powerful and good, even when bad things happen, because he is also all-knowing and sees how things work together for his glory. Instead of asking God to fit into my understanding, I needed to be the one to shift. For a long time, I was hesitant to even accept that realization as truth. I didn't want to shift; I wanted things to go my way. I wanted to control the situation, but I needed to shift my perspective to understand God's goodness more accurately according to what the Bible tells me about his character. As I understand God's goodness, considering my own suffering, the question isn't "Why did I suffer?" The question should be "Why has God given me so many extended periods that are *free* from grief and pain?" The fact that God has allowed me to have *any* good gift in this life is a testament to his abundant grace.

In his book *Gentle and Lowly*, author Dane Ortlund wrote, "The Christian life, from one angle, is the long journey of letting our natural assumption about who God is, over many decades, fall away, being slowly replaced with God's own insistence on who he is. This is hard work. It takes a lot of sermons and a lot of suffering to believe that God's deepest heart is merciful and gracious."[10]

Here Ortlund points to two things that can significantly serve our efforts to have true assumptions about who God is: sermons (absorbing the Bible) and suffering. Bible engagement and suffering have certainly been the most powerful forces in my life pointing me to a truer picture of God. When I let go of my assumptions, it allows me to see the character of God more clearly. And as we see him more clearly and know him more deeply, there is a critical shift in our perspective that allows our seeing more of eternity than the earthly.

I might not ever fully understand why we were given Ezra only to have to say goodbye. I suspect I'll always feel a reflexive ache in my heart when the memory of that child comes to mind.

Likewise, I will probably never really know why Zion had to face cancer. It was the most heart-wrenching experience of my life to watch her endure surgery, recovery, chemotherapy, and hospital stays where she was hooked up to what seemed like dozens of machines and IVs. But I do know that the day finally dawned during my little girl's remission when I saw the cancer for what it was—an opportunity for a more eternal focus.

One of my most frequently prayed prayers during the adoption process was that Michael and I would bond well with whichever child entered our home. I prayed for this time and again before we brought Zion home, and as we finally made the trip from China to the States with our daughter, we implemented the recommended steps from experts so that bonding and attachment would be strong. Walking through Zion's cancer focused Michael's and my attention on Zion in a unique and profound way. As I step back and look at Zion's cancer journey, with a renewed perspective I can see how the experience was, in part, an answer to my prayer for bonding.

For months we sat by Zion's side constantly, we both stayed every night in the hospital with her, we took care of her, we held her when she cried and hurt during surgery recovery and chemo, we made her comfortable, we decorated her room with pictures of the happier days when we'd first become a family, and we did everything we could to love and care for her well. With the effects of chemotherapy weakening her immune system, we also had a prolonged time of quarantine where we didn't go anywhere or see anyone, choosing instead to remain home together, alone.

Once we started venturing back into the world during the early days of her remission, people commented on how strong our family bond seemed. I couldn't help but agree. God had answered my prayer for a strong bond with Zion at least in part via cancer and all its travails.

More meaningful still, he had invited us as a family into deeper levels of intimacy with him as we allowed ourselves to see the whole situation as part of his perfect and glorious plan.

A CHANCE TO COLLECT YOUR THOUGHTS

Sit with your thoughts before God for a few minutes, paying attention to how you're feeling as you read each question to yourself. Take as much time as you need before moving on in the book.

Seeking God's Perspective in Our Pain

1. What are a few of the "switches" you've experienced along the way, times when life as you knew it shifted, seemingly in an instant? What were the circumstances involved, and how did you respond?
2. Do you make a practice of reading and knowing Scripture? Why or why not? Do you wish you had a deeper foundational knowledge of the Bible? What might that deeper foundation afford you?
3. What types of temporal preoccupations tend to captivate your attention and take your gaze off God? Would you consider these things idols? Why or why not?

CHAPTER 11

PERSEVERANCE

Staying the Course

Who has a harder fight than he who is
striving to overcome himself?

—THOMAS Á KEMPIS

MICHAEL

Whenever a stressful situation shows up in my life, I fall into a worst-case-scenario state of mind. Do you do this too, this *catastrophizing* thing? In truth, I don't really think that my life will end in disaster; it's just that I feel compelled to be prepared, just in case.

In my defense, sometimes this approach is a useful tack to take. For example, whenever I am nervous before speaking to a group, it's useful to remember that the worst thing that could happen is my talk goes horribly wrong and I trip walking off the stage. If I feel anxious in an interview or leading up to an important conversation, it's useful to remember that the worst thing that could happen is I look foolish to a person. If there is an investment I am unsure of, it's useful to remember that the worst thing that could happen is I lose the money invested. For the mundane anxieties of life, contemplating the worst-case scenario can be a great help. But when it comes to more consequential issues, it threatens to do me in.

Maturity for the Win

Lauren and I committed James 1:2–4 to memory in high school, and since then the words in those verses have served as a lifeline when things feel hard. Here's what it says: "Consider it pure joy, my brothers and sisters, whenever you face trials of many kinds, because you know that the testing of your faith produces perseverance. Let perseverance finish its work so that you may be mature and complete, not lacking anything." I was initially drawn to the wisdom that appeared to be so applicable to everyday life, but now the passage strikes me in a fresh way. The words have shifted from being theoretical to deeply experiential. I must admit, throughout various seasons, whenever I was denied the life I thought I was entitled to, experiencing "pure joy" was the furthest thing from my mind.

But even given my annoyance at the feeling that I was expected to cheer in response to calamity, I instinctively gravitated toward the promise posed on its heels: perfection, completion, lacking nothing. The idea of being steadfast was something I longed for in my life.

For a long time those verses messed with my mind. It felt absurd to accept the idea that the more trials you endured, the less you'd lack in life. To consider trials as something joyful felt like a stretch. But isn't that what the passage says? To understand spiritual truths, we need spiritual eyes to see. We need not a natural perspective but a divine one. We need not our own but God's take on things.

While I'm sure it is true that worst-case thinking can lead a person down some dark paths, for the believer in Jesus—according to James 1:2–4, anyway—the "worst-case scenario" in any form of suffering is a reality that is "mature" and "complete." In the words of C. S. Lewis, "In grief nothing 'stays put.' One keeps emerging from a phase, but it always recurs. Round and round. Everything repeats. Am I going in circles, or dare I hope I am on a spiral? But if a spiral, am I going up or down it?"[1]

Here's what all this means: When we're faced with difficult

circumstances, we can spiral downward to misery, increasingly sure that God is a sadist, that life is cruel, and that hopelessness is our fate. Or we can spiral upward to maturity, believing with ever-greater conviction that God will support that which he has ordained, that life is purposeful, and that our ultimate destination is a place of contentment, completeness, and peace.

As to which direction our spiral will head, the determining factor is perseverance. Thankfully, it's a skill we can hone.

Wisdom That's Not of This World

Lauren and I are both positive people, future-oriented people, people who love to learn. In the Japanese culture the term *kaizen*—a compound of two words literally meaning "good change"—is synonymous with the idea of continuous improvement. It's the idea that instead of spending time and energy fretting about the past and all that didn't happen just right, you press forward, anticipating something that has yet to come, something that just might be even better than you'd hoped it would be. That's us—to a tee. When bad things happen, we both reflexively reframe them. "I'm sure God will use this for good somehow," I say (once I've catastrophized, that is). "Yep," Lauren says, not missing a beat. "This will be used somehow."

She's the achiever; I'm the adventurer. Together, we're go, go, go. Diversion? No worries. Setback? No problem. Awful set of circumstances descending on us like a ton of bricks? No need to lose our cool over this. Keep moving. Keep hoping. Keep believing. Keep trying. God will use it for good somehow.

And yet even she and I, ever the go-getters, nearly lost our get-up-and-go along the way. Do you know the song "Nonstop" from the musical *Hamilton*? In it Aaron Burr asks Alexander Hamilton why he lives like he is always short on time. That unyielding sense of urgency pervades nearly everything Lauren and I do. So, yes, based on how life works, we expected obstacles along the way. We expected challenges—some perhaps even big. We just didn't expect them to never end.

As we entered the adoption process we expected to endure a difficult but brief season of childlessness but then receive the life that we desired. Instead we received not just detours but dead ends. Or so it has seemed to us.

If you keep reading in James 1 past the passage we looked at previously, you'll see that verse 5 says this: "If any of you lacks wisdom, you should ask God, who gives generously to all without finding fault, and it will be given to you."

Lauren and I have personalities that are bent toward optimism, activity, and moving ahead. But even those bright and sunny natural tendencies couldn't see us through to the end. We needed an infusion of supernatural wisdom. We needed God to weigh in on things.

For us, and for you as well, we simply cannot learn to count trials as joy until we first choose to count on God. The fact is that change changes us. God longs to change us through change. But we will never be changed unless we trust him to see us through. "We resist the change not because we can't accept the change," wrote William Bridges, a mastermind on the subject of life's transitions, "but because we can't accept letting go of that piece of ourselves that we have to give up when and because the situation has changed."[2]

WE SIMPLY CANNOT LEARN TO COUNT TRIALS AS JOY UNTIL WE FIRST CHOOSE TO COUNT ON GOD.

In other words, we won't admit that we're not in control.

As we face suffering of any kind—and the necessary change it brings—it's as if God stands before us, hand outstretched, and says, "The next version of you—the version that exists on the other side of this change—will be better still."

When we cede control and trust God to see us through that season, in effect, we nod and take his hand.

Knowing and Loving

Before Lauren and I got married, we read a fantastic book by Gary Thomas titled *Sacred Marriage*, and the biggest takeaway for us both was the author's assertion that the goal of marriage isn't for our happiness but for our holiness. Let's sit here for just a second while I absorb that reality again and you absorb it perhaps for the first time.

Holiness.

Not happiness.

This is not what I'd seen occur in most of the marriages I'd seen as a kid. For starters, I'd watched my own parents' marriage fall apart, purportedly because of confusion over this very thing.

I was determined to do better.

I *had* to do better in my marriage.

The goal is holiness.

The goal is holiness.

The goal is holiness.

If I ever get a tattoo, it will be those four words on my skin. Well, that, or the logo for OU.

Now, because the marriage covenant reflects Jesus' (the groom's) relationship with his church (the bride), Thomas's work also helped me reinforce proper expectations for what it means to follow Christ. Here's a mindblower, if ever there were one: followers of Jesus rightly follow Jesus not to be made happy but to be made holy.

The goal in our suffering is holiness as well.

And how are we to be made holy? By following the example of Christ. And in following Christ, we find a greater happiness than anything this world has to offer. True holiness ultimately leads to our happiness. When we pursue happiness outside of holiness, we get neither. When we pursue holiness to gain happiness, we receive both.

If you are walking through a painful season right now and feel your resolve slipping, even as you long to stay the course, let me give you three considerations to sit with, three certainties to nail down in your life. The first one is this: *be sure you know Jesus.*

Be Sure You Know Jesus

We can't rightly view the trials we face without first having a right relationship with God. We can't mature in our faith without first activating that faith by trusting Christ. We can't be governed by divine wisdom until divinity is operational in our lives. And so, to learn to persevere, we must first be certain that we know the ultimate example of perseverance: Jesus himself.

In his letter to the church in Rome, the apostle Paul wrote, "Brothers and sisters, my heart's desire and prayer to God for the Israelites is that they may be saved" (Romans 10:1). Several verses later, he then explained what it means to be saved: "If you declare with your mouth, 'Jesus is Lord,' and believe in your heart that God raised him from the dead, you will be saved. For it is with your heart that you believe and are justified, and it is with your mouth that you profess your faith and are saved" (vv. 9–10).

Confession. Belief. That's it.

Back when I first created my Facebook account (when college students were the only ones allowed on the platform), users could enter personal information such as where they lived, what their interests were, and whom they were dating.

Linking your account to someone you were dating was a key step in a relationship, one that made you "Facebook official." Back then, you could enter your religious beliefs the same way. In light of this verse, mine simply read "Jesus is Lord." I figured if there were any doubt in heaven, I could just point to my profile and tell God I was covered. It was Facebook official, after all.

In verse 13, Paul reiterated how one surrenders to the lordship of Jesus by quoting the prophet Joel, who said, "And everyone who calls on the name of the Lord will be saved; for on Mount Zion and in Jerusalem there will be deliverance, as the Lord has said, even among the survivors whom the Lord calls" (Joel 2:32).

To access the resources that come with knowing Jesus, you must first know who he is.

Be Sure You're Following Jesus

Here's the second consideration: *be sure you're following Jesus.*

While we were in the thick of Zion's cancer journey, one of my closest friends—and a confessing Christian, I should mention—walked through a situation that no married man ever wants to go through: his wife left him. But here's the thing: she left him because he was being a chronic jerk. This wasn't her opinion; I'm a longtime friend to the guy, and even I told him to his face (several times) that he was, in fact, being a jerk: selfish, inconsiderate, mean. At the beginning of this chapter, I said that when faced with hardship, we can either spiral downward toward misery or spiral upward toward maturity, and it absolutely broke my heart to watch my friend choose misery's path. He backed out of our friendship. He left the church. He let his wife leave. And he hopped on that awful spiral like it was a ride at Disney World and held on as tight as he could.

I reached out to him and begged him to reconsider his ways. I prayed fervently for him during that season, that he would wake up and reverse his course. But that just wasn't to be. Convinced that there was no point in working on his marriage, my friend signed all the paperwork and moved on.

Let me ask you the question I asked myself a thousand times during those days: Was my friend "following Jesus" as he pursued the path he took?

Only God knows—that's the sole answer here. My purpose in raising the question isn't necessarily to solicit an answer. It's simply to invite you and me to practice asking ourselves the same thing. In the thoughts we choose to entertain and the words we choose to speak and the actions we choose to take, are we following Jesus or the way of the world?

In Galatians 5:25, Paul wrote, "Since we live by the Spirit, [meaning that we have come into a saving relationship with Jesus], let us keep in step with the Spirit." In other words, don't merely believe in God; even the demons believe in God (James 2:19). We must also behave as we believe. According to the preceding verses in Galatians 5, here's how we can do just that:

> So I say, walk by the Spirit, and you will not gratify the desires of the flesh. For the flesh desires what is contrary to the Spirit,

> and the Spirit what is contrary to the flesh. They are in conflict with each other, so that you are not to do whatever you want. But if you are led by the Spirit, you are not under the law. The acts of the flesh are obvious: sexual immorality, impurity and debauchery; idolatry and witchcraft; hatred, discord, jealousy, fits of rage, selfish ambition, dissensions, factions and envy; drunkenness, orgies, and the like. I warn you, as I did before, that those who live like this will not inherit the kingdom of God. But the fruit of the Spirit is love, joy, peace, forbearance, kindness, goodness, faithfulness, gentleness and self-control. Against such things there is no law. (vv. 16–23)

When we look at the life and legacy of Jesus, these traits—love, joy, goodness, patience, and all the rest—are the characteristics that stand out. Unlike any person ever to live, Jesus reflected perfect synchronicity with the Spirit of God. As the sinless One, he was incapable of being sexually immoral, impure, idolatrous, habitually filled with rage, and so forth. Yes, he was tempted as you and I are tempted today. But not once did he fall into sin.

I pause here to reinforce this point because a Barna study that still haunts me stated that while roughly 75 percent of Americans claim to be Christians, half of those "believers" do not believe that Jesus lived a sinless life.[3] (Worse yet? Half of that half only agree "somewhat" that he was without sin.) This means that in this country we have a larger lost demographic among the falsely converted than among those who would say outright that they do not believe in God. Here's what I'm compelled to remind us: if we don't believe in a Jesus who didn't sin, then we believe in a Jesus who can't save us from sin—a perilous prospect indeed.

I know it's popular to cherry-pick Bible verses to live by and to disregard the rest, but let me give you a passage that is absolutely worth your careful attention, memorization, and study:

> For to this [meaning the exhortation in verse 19 to endure sorrows while suffering unjustly by being mindful of God] you have been called, because Christ also suffered for you, leaving you an example, so that you might follow in his steps. He committed no sin, neither was deceit found in his mouth. When he was reviled, he did not revile in return; when he suffered, he did not threaten, but continued entrusting himself to him who judges justly. He himself bore our sins in his body on the tree, that we might die to sin and live to righteousness. By his wounds you have been healed. For you were straying like sheep, but have now returned to the Shepherd and Overseer of your souls. (1 Peter 2:21–25 ESV)

We see the truth of these verses in all four of the Gospels, when Jesus is found hanging on a Roman cross, being crucified for wrongs he did not commit. He took on that full burden of sinfulness—including your sin and mine—begging his heavenly Father not for justice but to forgive his murderers that day.

In short, he persevered. He insisted on staying the course. Fixing his gaze on the resurrection to come instead of on his present pain, he endured that great agony, he died for our sins, and he defeated nothing short of death. He did what you and I can also do in that he redirected his attention from the temporally awful to the eternally beautiful. He set his sights on that. Jerry Bridges addressed this issue in his magnificent work *Trusting God*: "The Christian life is intended to be one of continuous growth. We all want to grow, but we often resist the process. This is because we tend to focus on the events of the adversity themselves, rather than looking with the eye of faith beyond the events to what God is doing in our lives."[4]

When we believe in Jesus and demonstrate our love for him by faithfully following his example, being mindful of all that he has done for us, we are able to persevere. We trust that the same God who ordained that his only begotten Son die a humiliating death for the sake of all humankind has ordained our suffering here and now. And that the same God who used that great sacrifice of Jesus to pave a path between himself and man will use our suffering for good somehow, that he'll make things all right in the end.

THE SAME GOD WHO USED THAT GREAT SACRIFICE OF JESUS TO PAVE A PATH BETWEEN HIMSELF AND MAN WILL USE OUR SUFFERING FOR GOOD SOMEHOW.

I quoted this verse silently as I listened to my friend Kevin telling me yesterday that he hadn't gotten the job he wanted, the job he'd applied for with confidence to spare. In the moment, I was tempted to say, "There's something better out there for you," but thankfully, I caught myself. "There's something out there for you," I said instead. I said it because it was true. The promise of the gospel isn't that by believing in God and following Jesus, we will be granted our every wish. On the contrary, we are promised we will "have trouble" in this world, as we saw already when we looked at John 16:33. The promise is that when things all come together, in light of eternity and the glory of God, the culmination will be good even if life gets harder. For Kevin, for me, for you as well, that "coming together" may include a little suffering or a lot—I don't know. But it will be a chosen life. A predestined life. A providential life in Christ.

God says he'll work things together for our good, and those on the spiral upward toward spiritual maturity are determined to take him at his word.

Begin Again When You Fail

A third and final consideration: *give yourself grace when you fail.*

One of my favorite aspects of the Bible is that God saw fit to include both sides of the ledger when depicting the reality of human life. We see the assets, we see the liabilities, we see it all. And from both types of examples, we can learn.

On this subject of perseverance, think about the Bible figures of Judas Iscariot and Simon Peter. Let's look first at the similarities between the two. Both lived in the first century. Both were Jewish. Both were early disciples of Jesus during his earthly ministry. Same, same, same. But when each of these men faced failure in the face of Jesus, their paths dramatically diverged.

Judas's downfall began when as the disciples' treasurer he seemingly became more enamored of money than of Christ. John 12:1–7 tells the story of Jesus and some of his disciples enjoying dinner in the home of their friends, siblings Mary, Martha, and Lazarus, when Mary approached Jesus and anointed his feet with a pound of perfumed ointment. As she wiped the balm from his feet with her hair, the fragrance filled the air.

In three of the four gospels we read that one of the disciples spoke up, asking why on earth Mary would do such a thing, when that costly ointment could have been sold for money, which could have then been given to the poor. Only in the book of John do we learn that that disciple was Judas. John then offered a note of commentary on Judas's move, saying, "He did not say this because he cared about the poor but because he [Judas] was a thief; as keeper of the money bag, he used to help himself to what was put into it" (John 12:6).

Make of John's statement what you will, but future events would seem to echo this supposed greed.

But what of Simon Peter? We meet Simon Peter just after his younger brother Andrew first encountered Jesus. Andrew ran to alert Peter that he had "found the Messiah" (John 1:41). He then brought Peter to Jesus, who said, "You are Simon son of John. You will be called Cephas (which, when translated, is Peter)" (v. 42). Soon thereafter, Jesus came to Peter's home to heal Peter's mother-in-law, who often stayed with her daughter and son-in-law. Peter was the one who famously tried to walk on water after seeing Jesus successfully doing the same. He openly confessed Jesus as Lord, saying, "You are the Messiah, the Son of the living God" (Matthew 16:16). By all accounts, Peter was considered part of Jesus' inner circle of friends and seemed genuinely intent on both understanding and following Jesus' way. (I'm thinking here of the scene when Peter asked Jesus about forgiveness in Matthew 18. Maybe he was trying to get out of forgiving a chronic offender, but hey, at least he asked.)

Peter was no doubt a real-deal human, someone who sometimes misspoke, sometimes misstepped, and sometimes napped at exactly the wrong time (Matthew 26:40–43). But here's where Peter got things right: on the heels of the greatest mistake in his life, the falling away that for all of history would become synonymous with his name, he returned to Jesus, the one he had wronged, and decided to begin again.

Just before Jesus prayed in the garden of Gethsemane for God to remove his cup of suffering from him and was subsequently arrested and then killed, Jesus foretold to his disciples that they would all fall away from him that night, that they all would fail to persevere. Peter was among those in the crowd and was offended by this statement. "Even if all fall away on account of you," Peter said, "I never will" (Matthew 26:33).

Jesus looked at Peter and confirmed what he had said: "'Truly I tell you,' Jesus answered, 'this very night, before the rooster crows, you will disown me three times'" (v. 34).

Peter couldn't take it anymore. Looking straight at Jesus, he said, "Even if I have to die with you, I will never disown you" (v. 35).

And wouldn't you know it, that in the very same chapter of Scripture, those three denials unfold, one by one. A servant girl approached Peter, asking if he had been with Jesus. "I don't know what you're talking about," he said (v. 70). Another servant girl said to the crowd, "This fellow was with Jesus of Nazareth," to which Peter said, "I don't know the man!" (vv. 71–72). A while later, bystanders came to Peter, saying, "Surely you are one of them," to which Peter swore he did not know Jesus Christ (v. 73).

Denial one. Denial two. Denial three. And then the rooster crowed.

When we left Judas, he was complaining about Mary's financial mismanagement of that costly ointment, saying that of course if it had been up to him, he'd have sold the perfume and given the money to the poor. But soon enough, he was reclined at the table enjoying the Last Supper with Jesus, when Jesus told the men that one of them would betray him.

Simon Peter poked John and told him to ask Jesus who it was. "Jesus answered, 'It is the one to whom I will give this piece of bread when I have dipped it in the dish.' Then, dipping the piece of bread, he gave it to Judas, the son of Simon Iscariot" (John 13:26). The text says that after Judas took the morsel from Jesus, "Satan entered into him" (v. 27).

It should come as no real surprise when we get to the garden of Gethsemane, where Jesus was praying, we find a band of soldiers seeking to arrest him. Here was the betrayal Jesus foretold; Judas had tipped them off. "Who is it you want?" Jesus asked the soldiers, to which they said, "Jesus of Nazareth" (John 18:4–5). Jesus was then detained.

It's easy to lose Judas's plot from that point forward because the events of the resurrection are so weighty and all-encompassing, but it's critical to note that as Jesus was standing trial before Pontius Pilate, the Roman governor who would eventually order Jesus' crucifixion, Judas had second thoughts about his role in how things went down. Matthew 27:3–5 reads this way:

> When Judas, who had betrayed him, saw that Jesus was condemned, he was seized with remorse and returned the thirty pieces of silver to the chief priests and the elders. "I have sinned," he said, "for I have betrayed innocent blood."
>
> "What is that to us?" they replied. "That's your responsibility."
>
> So Judas threw the money into the temple and left. Then he went away and hanged himself.

Following the Gospels, the book of Acts opens with Judas being replaced by Matthias, Jesus' new disciple, and with a wiser, more reflective Simon Peter astutely delivering the sermon of his life. We know from John's gospel that following the resurrection, Jesus restored Peter, asking three times if he loved him—one time for each denial. And now, in the book of Acts, Peter was used by God to draw countless thousands to himself—God was glorified mightily through this man.

Do you see it? It's the spiral we looked at before. Trials will put us all on a spiral, but we get to choose where it goes. That spiral can move downward toward abject misery or upward toward spiritual maturity. We can persevere in our faith—or not.

Direction, Not Perfection

When I was a teenager and found out that my parents were getting a divorce, I walked through a pretty dark season of doubt. I'd been saved and baptized as a young elementary school kid, I'd grown up in the church, and admittedly things had been pretty idyllic for my family and me until that terrible turn of events. But as my family fractured, I remember feeling iffy about God. Could he really be trusted to help me keep it together when he'd so clearly failed my mom and dad? I wasn't so sure.

There's a story in the Bible that comes to mind just now, of a man who desperately wanted to persevere but was having trouble staying the course. His son had been possessed by an evil spirit since childhood, and now Jesus was standing before the father, all healing in the palm of his hand. The father said, "It [the spirit] has often thrown him into fire or water to kill him. But if you can do anything, take pity on us and help us" (Mark 9:22), to which Jesus, no doubt unimpressed by the man's lack of faith, said, "'If you can'? . . . Everything is possible for one who believes" (v. 23). The man, now exposed, looked at Jesus and cried out, "I do believe; help me overcome my unbelief!" (v. 24).

I've been there; how about you?

Maybe you're there right now. You want to believe but you can't. Life is just making it too hard. If I were to offer a piece of advice, it would be this: believe God as long as you are able, and as soon as you can believe him no longer, simply tell him so. Do exactly what this man did: look Jesus right in the eye, declare your deep-seated belief, and then beg God to restore it for you. God loves to answer that prayer.

And in the meantime, keep talking to more mature believers. Keep praying to your heavenly Father, regardless of whether you think he's listening to you. Keep reading your Bible, day after day, letting its truths soak into your heart. When Lauren was a sophomore in high school, she decided that before graduation she was going to read though the entire Bible cover to cover. This was no small task, given how occupied she was with schoolwork, playing basketball, her internship with her family's business, and a busy social life. But she did it—she got all the way through. And to this day, she says it was one of the most meaningful spiritual experiences she's ever had. It was meaningful not because she memorized a whole slew of verses, although she did memorize a few. It was meaningful because she saw the heart of God for what it was: compassionate, loving, good.

He wants you to know his heart too. Come. Come and read, pray, listen, learn, and stay, trusting that the blessings of perseverance will come to you for the simple fact that you've persevered.

Letting the Shaping Occur

About six years into our fruitless adoption journey, Lauren and I quit talking with friends and family members about our goal to adopt. We were getting worn out from answering the typical questions regarding how things were progressing, mostly because things weren't progressing at all. After years of articulating a thousand versions of "Nothing yet," we fell silent on the subject and hoped our relational circle would move on.

When a woman gets pregnant, most of the time she and her

husband will bring a baby into the world in about nine months. For Lauren and me, reality wasn't as predictable as that. Instead, it was like, "Yeah, we've filed our paperwork. And so now we're hoping to have a kid in . . . I don't know—a decade?"

We had been told by the agency that it would take twelve to twenty-four months to be matched with and bring home our child. That was encouraging news, as we did the math and told ourselves that by the second half of 2019, we should plan on traveling to pick up our newborn baby. But that plan wasn't to be.

In January 2019, our social worker called with news: "Things aren't happening in China. The program's slowing down."

They told us it would be an additional six months to our expected wait time. Mm-hmm. Fool us once, and all that.

I should mention that this was happening on the heels of being told that the first plan we'd pursued for years—adopting from Uganda—wasn't going to pan out. These delays were beyond annoying. We were ready to move.

Lauren and I, along with several other families, were asked to join a conference call with the agency for the purpose of having the delays more thoroughly explained. It would be a forty-five-minute call, and then they would take questions. After the main portion of the meeting had ended, the wife of one of the other couples unmuted herself and said with more than a little annoyance in her tone, "You know, we've already been in the process for seven months. How much longer are we going to have to wait?"

I knew I was also unmuted, but frankly, I didn't care. I laughed aloud—unapologetically so. Seven months? They were crying foul after seven *months*? We'd been at it for six years. Talk about running out of time!

Later that night, Lauren and I sat down in the living room to debrief the day, and the call came up. I said something flippant

about the nerve of that woman to gripe about seven lousy months, but Lauren didn't take the bait. She sat there silently for a beat and then looked at me and said, "I know. But seven months is still seven months. That's seven months of hoping and waiting and praying and wanting to believe that they will one day have a child."

I didn't want to hear that then. But now, I'm thinking about how great it is that I married such a wise woman.

I can finally see that the time that God took in placing Zion in our care was the right amount of time. I needed to grow. I needed to mature. I needed to keep trusting him, even in the dark. I needed to confirm my belief that he is always up to something good.

Having Z with us? It's very, very good.

The brilliant essayist, teacher, and thinker David Powlison, self-described as a "stubborn" convert to Christianity during his college days at Harvard University in the 1960s, wrote in his book *God's Grace in Your Suffering*,

> God will surprise you. He will make you stop. You will struggle. He will bring you up short. You will hurt. He will take his time. You will grow in faith and in love. He will deeply delight you. You will find the process harder than you ever imagined—and better. Goodness and mercy will follow you all the days of your life. At the end of the long road you will come home at last.[5]

Mr. Powlison died one year later, but not before those words surely ministered to every reader who encountered them. To find the deepest of struggles and the deepest of delights in the same divine Source would seem like the height of paradox if we didn't understand the character of God.

Thankfully we can understand his character.
When we immerse ourselves in his Word, thankfully we *do*.
We really can learn to count trials as joyful.
For those intent on persevering, we must.

A CHANCE TO COLLECT YOUR THOUGHTS

Sit with your thoughts before God for a few minutes, paying attention to how you're feeling as you read each question to yourself. Take as much time as you need before moving on in the book.

What Jesus' Example of Perseverance Means for Us

1. How does it sit with you that based on what James 1:2–4 says we can consider our trials "pure joy"?
2. Do you agree or disagree with the idea that walking with God has more to do with our holiness than with our happiness? Why?
3. Why do you suppose that the call for believers is to behave as we believe?

CONCLUSION

Where Do We Go from Here?

The victory of Jesus Christ, his kingdom, and his glory, come by way of the scars, by weakness, by suffering.

DIANE LANGBERG

MICHAEL

It was early November 2022, and while the air in Oklahoma was still warm, my wife climbed into the attic to pull out the Christmas decorations. You may be of the mindset that Christmas decorations have no place in the house until after Thanksgiving, but around here we aim for November 1. Or Lauren does, anyway. But given the sheer delight this process brings her, I go along for the ride. You might say she comes by it honestly, seeing as in Hobby Lobby stores all over this country, Christmas decor gets staged in *June*.

Summer had ended, taking its scorching temperatures with it, and while I was grateful for the cooler air, a sense of dread still rose. Cooler temps meant fall and winter, winter meant the Christmas holiday season, and December 17 meant the anniversary of losing our son. I didn't want the sting of pain and intensity of grief that I was sure that anniversary would bring.

With that anniversary on the horizon, I figured Lauren and I should seek any bit of enjoyment we could find. After helping her pack away the Halloween decor, I carried boxes of Christmas trees down, praying that the mere sight of them would lighten the mood. It didn't.

I watched as Lauren carefully assembled the various trees, eight in all, positioning them just so in the living room, creating something of a winter forest scene. She plugged in the lights, stood back to survey the warm glow, and fixed a smile to her face. But behind her smile, I could see it: that gnawing sense of sadness that was rearing its ugly head.

Moving Forward Despite Our Pain

I've got to hand it to her: despite the pain, she pressed forward, determined to get the job done, but days later, as she sat alone on a flight to a speaking engagement, she could stuff her grief no longer, and it was then she burst into tears.

When we lost Ezra, it was eight days before Christmas. We'd been surrounded by the sights and sounds of the most wonderful time of the year, and now that he was gone, nothing felt wonderful to us.

The familiar sights and sounds brought with it the traumatic nature of what had happened in its setting: saying goodbye to our son, packing his bag to hand him over to someone, telling our daughter she wouldn't see him again, all while sitting in our living room with the warm glow of our Christmas tree forest. Now those glowing lights only brought back the deep cut of pain and darkness of our loss. I thought about Zion holding her little brother on that very couch, shocked when the little man's razor-sharp nails accidentally grazed Zion's tender cheek. "Oww, brother!" Zion had hollered while Lauren tugged tiny socks over Ezra's hands. "There you go, sugar," she'd said.

We couldn't have known that our collective pain would cut far deeper than that, as days became weeks, which turned into months.

I am struck by the fact that today as I write this, it is the one-year anniversary of Ezra's departure. On this day exactly twelve months ago, I walked upstairs and opened the door of our son's room to see him standing in his crib smiling back at me. I picked him up, gave him a peck on the cheek, and whispered into his soft, tiny ear as I had every day since we'd met. "Good morning, buddy," I said. He wriggled happily in my arms, all buzzy with baby energy and enthusiasm for whatever adventure was coming next. That would be the last morning I ever held Ezra, kissed him, whispered my love straight into his soul.

We think we can know what to expect out of life, out of people, and out of situations. But life throws us curveballs, we experience loss, failures happen, relationships turn sour, sickness shows up, and babies are taken away. We wish we could control our lives and the people and circumstances in them. But the more we press in on control, the less stable we feel as our own inability to really control things is inevitably revealed.

But increasingly I'm asking myself the question I invite you to ponder, which is, Even if we could have such control, are we sure we would steward it well?

I know how fallen I am, and deep down I know how dangerous that kind of power would be in the hands of a fallen world. That power can be entrusted only to a perfect, good, and just God. That is what we have in our heavenly Father, a God who will never betray us, even if in our pain it doesn't feel that way. A God who loves us, who sees us, who created us, who has good in mind for us for eternity.

God loves us so much that he gave his only Son so that he might have a relationship with me and with you. I have a God who can sympathize with Lauren and me in the loss of our son, because he willingly gave up his for us. Because God is perfect, holy, and just, he can't be in the presence of the imperfect. This means that for us to have the relationship we have, there had to be a perfect sacrifice to pay the penalty of our sin so that we could be made right. That's what Christ did in leaving heaven to come to earth. Jesus lived a perfect life and then took our place on the cross as he died for our sin. For those who call on Jesus, claim forgiveness of sin, and surrender to God, they are now seen by God through the lens of Christ's sufficient sacrifice, of his righteousness and holiness, of grace. This free gift of salvation, the hope of the gospel, the character of our heavenly Father—this is what we cling to when life isn't going the way we hoped or planned.

A Word to the Friend of One Who Is Hurting

Life will bring all kinds of hardships into our lives and the lives of those we love. You may have come to this book seeking insight not for yourself but because you are walking alongside someone who is in a dark season. Our hope is that as you have journeyed with us, you've been able to catch glimpses of the pain points that others might be experiencing and that you have benefited from the ways we have considered what might bring hope and comfort as you walk alongside them.

The Bible often reminds us that we were made for relationships. At the core of our identity as image bearers of the triune God who had community among himself (Genesis 1:26–27), we see this innate need in ourselves for relationships. For believers, as we looked at previously, we are also instructed to be in relationship with one another to bear one another's burdens (Galatians 6:2). At face value it sounds like a nice calling to take up part of the burden another person may be bearing. Experientially and personally, it is a much harder thing to find the willingness to lean down and take up that burden with your fellow traveler in life, because it often means many aspects of your own world will be disrupted.

As Lauren and I have learned, tragedies and hardships never happen on time. Hardships invade our calendar and turn life upside down. To step into the chaos of a person's disrupted life is to value that person over our own calendar, comfort, and convenience—100 percent of the time.

Saying yes to being with someone facing hardship means being willing to see others in their pain. For the person walking in grief, it means sitting with them as they cry, letting them talk, and giving them time to move through their pain at the pace that serves them best. This is what sacrificial love demands: that we set aside our own needs, our own inclination to only look on the bright side, our impulse to give correction at the wrong time, and our urge to find solutions, choosing instead to be present. Flexible. Patient. Kind. Showing this type of empathy and love models the heart of our Emmanuel, God with us.

Our Calling

Our Savior was a "man of sorrows"—as the prophet called him in Isaiah 53:3—who sat with the broken and who calls us to follow him. Jesus Christ left the comfort of heaven to live a life here on earth. He was fully God, yet he was fully human. If we are to follow in the footsteps of Christ, we must step into the suffering of this world and its plentiful pain—both our own and that of others—in his name. In so doing, we bring the gospel to a fellow sufferer in a real and tangible way. As we sit with someone in their pain, give them the space and freedom to weep, show them we will support them through prayer, and provide empathy to their pain, we provide an example of the loving-kindness of our heavenly Father and perhaps open the door to further conversation regarding how Christ entered the darkness of our world and brought light through his death and resurrection. He first sat with people, ate with those whose hearts were broken, listened to the hurting, and found fellowship with sinners.

All suffering will, in the end, be temporal. That is, except for the suffering for sin borne for all eternity, experienced by those who do not have salvation through the gospel and thus will be permanently separated from God.[1] As we are called to follow Christ's footsteps into the darkness, we are also called to point to his eternal light. We live the gospel, and we also speak the gospel. We share of his truth and forgiveness because it is the only true healing we can receive. The gospel is the only hope that matters—both now and for eternity.

Our purpose in life is to glorify God. Our suffering, or the suffering of others, doesn't alter that reality. Christ left the glory of heaven when he came to earth, and his life on earth brought greater glory to the Father through his obedience. Just as Christ entered our world for the sake of our lives, we enter others' for the sake of being an incarnated representation of the gospel of Jesus Christ and his great love.

Entering into the pain of others, whether it looks like walking alongside someone battling cancer, stepping in to care for a foster child coming out of a stressful environment, finding resources for a friend who is battling addiction, providing support to a woman facing an unplanned pregnancy in challenging circumstances, building a relationship with a resettled refugee from a war-torn country, as you enter another's pain, not only will you facilitate positive change in the other person but you yourself will be changed.

Lauren and I have experienced firsthand the transformation of walking alongside others. As mentioned in chapter 5, our close friends Landry and Kayla had their twin boys and had to say goodbye to them shortly after we said goodbye to Ezra. Walking with them through their pain has been healing and validating for us because our experiences are different, but our desires are the same. We long to see God use this sorrow in our lives to maximize our joy in him.

We enter the darkness because Christ entered our darkness and brought life (John 1:1–5). Christ brought truth and love. He brought hope and healing. Christ neither abandoned us nor took on the darkness of sin, even while in his suffering he took on the punishment we deserved for our sin. And if Christ's obedience led to his suffering and brought greater glory, we can trust that our obedience to God, while it may lead to suffering in our own lives, will ultimately bring him glory. In the process, we open ourselves up to more of him.

With the promise of Emmanuel—literally, "God with us"—we have his presence with us during our earthly days and all the hope, peace, joy, and comfort that he brings, yet we also have the hope of our future with God in eternity, when all troubles and trauma disappear. In eternity we won't need to grasp for control to have peace. We'll simply marvel at God's glory as we live whole and holy lives.

As I've experienced pain, suffering, and the loss of control in my own life, as well as by walking alongside others who have encountered trials, there are some passages in Scripture I can no longer read without my eyes welling up with tears. Revelation 21:1–4, with its reference to our new heaven and new earth where God will wipe away every tear, is one of those passages.

IN ETERNITY WE WON'T NEED TO GRASP FOR CONTROL TO HAVE PEACE. WE'LL SIMPLY MARVEL AT GOD'S GLORY AS WE LIVE WHOLE AND HOLY LIVES.

What a hope we have, both for today with the promise of God's presence in our lives and for our future in eternity with him.

Dark Seasons, More Light

Once Lauren and I realized that our Christmas trees and decorations had been triggering flashbacks to our final days with Ezra, Lauren decided to mix things up by dispersing the trees, placing some in the dining room, some in the kitchen, some in different spots in the living room, and some in the bedrooms upstairs.

As for our main Christmas tree, after my mother-in-law heard us talking about the overwhelming emotions that the holidays were conjuring for us, she bought us a beautiful new Christmas tree that looked different from our previous one. This new tree stood tall as the perfect centerpiece of our home.

Admittedly, the new arrangements and the new tree did nothing to erase the pain of our loss. What they did do was help us to settle into this new way of seeing life. Grief may not ever "feel better," but it can feel *different*. The losses, hardships, trials, and pain we face make a conduit in our lives for us to find more intimacy and presence with God.

While the light from our Christmas trees used to be concentrated on only one space in our home, it now brings brightness into nearly every room. Pain does that for us. It provides the pathway for God to bring his light, comfort, and healing into new areas of our lives that might not have been given to him otherwise.

What a gift—the greatest gift of all—more of his light.

More of his life.

More of him.

ACKNOWLEDGMENTS

There are so many who have been with us through the journey of these pages and beyond, and we could never adequately thank everyone for the support we have felt. We do want to mention a number of people specifically though.

Our family, Steve and Jackie Green, Terri McAfee, Danielle and Caleb Smith, Lindy and Danny Johnson, Grace Green, Gabi Green, Derek and Erica Green, and Bear and Clytee McAfee for helping babysit Zion, Ezra, and Zara over the past couple of years while we found times to work on the book. You also stood by us in the darkest days and loved us so well. We could not have done it without you!

Thank you to our church family. We cannot imagine who we would be without the sweet community we have cherished at Council Road Baptist Church since we were kids. We cherish the deep and meaningful relationships we have there and the wildly talented staff and leaders who minister to us each week. There's no place like home.

To our friends and acquaintances near and far who have encouraged us, prayed for us, and been there to walk with us through a truly challenging season. We are so fortunate both to have received such kind support and for the loving people who have made all the difference in our lives.

Thank you to the two incredible leaders who have believed in this project and journeyed with us since the beginning. Lisa Jackson, you believed in us and the message of this book. Thank you for your encouragement, advocacy, and personal care as we processed our story. Janet Talbert, your guidance and editorial sharpening was indispensable. Thank you for tender and firm leadership throughout the writing of this book.

A very special acknowledgement to the late Ginger Kolbaba. While her time on earth was cut short before this project got underway, we will forever cherish the transcripts she captured of us processing our journey with Zion in March 2020, one week before the world shut down. Our deepest condolences to her family.

This book would not exist without the incredible partnership we enjoyed with Ash Wiersma. You truly have been the steady hand that kept us on time and on target. You possess an uncanny knack to select the ideal word or phrase from your extensive vocabulary at each turn. Thank you for pushing us to grow into better writers.

The entire team at Nelson has been a joy to work with over the past couple of years, especially Natalie Nyquist, John Andrade, Sarah Van Cleve, and Lisa Beech. We are incredibly honored to be a part of such a life-giving team.

We are grateful for our two daughters, Zion and Zara, who watched us pull out our laptops in the evenings as they were slipping away to bed. We can't believe how blessed we are to be their parents, and our journey into motherhood and fatherhood has shaped this book.

And of course, we are so grateful for you, Ez. Buddy, you have no idea how much we love you and how our hearts long for you every day. We begged God to let us be your forever family. God didn't just say no to our request but also said yes to his best. While a piece of us will always be incomplete here on earth, it will only serve to magnify the sweetness of the life to come. Our deepest prayer is that we are reunited with you in that place where all the sad things of life become untrue.

NOTES

Introduction

1. Ezra's name was legally changed after he left our family, but to protect his privacy we continue to refer to him as Ezra.

Chapter 1: Misconceptions

1. J. I. Packer, *A Quest for Godliness: The Puritan Vision of the Christian Life* (Wheaton, IL: Crossway, 1990), 126.
2. A. W. Tozer, *Knowledge of the Holy* (New York: Harper & Row, 1961), 1.
3. John Piper, *Providence* (Wheaton, IL: Crossway, 2020), 30.
4. Piper, *Providence*, 43.
5. C. S. Lewis, *Reflections on the Psalms* (1958; repr., New York: HarperOne, 2017), 108.
6. Lewis, *Reflections on the Psalms*, 110.

Chapter 2: Expectations

1. John Flavel, *The Mystery of Providence* (Philadelphia: Presbyterian Board of Publications, 1840), 146.
2. Charles H. Spurgeon, "The Best Beloved," in *Metropolitan Tabernacle Pulpit: Sermons Preached and Revised by C. H. Spurgeon, During the Year 1878*, vol. 24 (London: Passmore & Alabaster, 1880), https://www.spurgeon.org/resource-library/sermons/the-best-beloved/#flipbook/.
3. Flavel, *Mystery of Providence*, 84.

Chapter 3: Anxiety

1. Sharon Hodde Miller, *The Cost of Control: Why We Crave It, the Anxiety It Gives Us, and the Real Power God Promises* (Grand Rapids: MI: Baker Books, 2022), 30.
2. Miller, *Cost of Control*, 18.

3. Mary E. Duffy, Jean M. Twenge, and Thomas E. Joiner, "Trends in Mood and Anxiety Symptoms and Suicide-Related Outcomes Among U.S. Undergraduates, 2007–2018: Evidence from Two National Surveys," *Journal of Adolescent Health* 65, no. 5 (November 2019): 590–98, https://doi.org/10.1016/j.jadohealth.2019.04.033.
4. Timothy Keller, *Prayer: Experiencing Awe and Intimacy with God* (New York: Penguin Books, 2014), 219.
5. Timothy Keller (@timkellernyc), Twitter post, September 13, 2021, 6:11 a.m., https://twitter.com/timkellernyc/status/1437373245418876936?lang=en.
6. Dane Ortlund, *Gentle and Lowly: The Heart of Christ for Sinners and Sufferers* (Wheaton, IL: Crossway, 2020), 149.

Chapter 4: Grief

1. Bessel van der Kolk, *The Body Keeps the Score: Brain, Mind, and Body in the Healing of Trauma* (New York: Penguin Books, 2014).
2. "Fast Facts: Preventing Adverse Childhood Experiences," Centers for Disease Control and Prevention, reviewed April 6, 2022, https://www.cdc.gov/violenceprevention/aces/fastfact.html.
3. Kelly M. Kapic, *You're Only Human: How Your Limits Reflect God's Design and Why That's Good News* (Grand Rapids, MI: Brazos Press, 2022), 5.
4. N. T. Wright, "Five Things to Know About Lament," N. T. Wright Online, accessed May 2, 2023, https://www.ntwrightonline.org/five-things-to-know-about-lament/.
5. "Book of Lamentations Summary: Complete Animated Overview," Bible Project, June 30, 2016, YouTube video, 7:16, https://youtu.be/p8GDFPdaQZQ.
6. Diane Langberg, *Suffering and the Heart of God: How Trauma Destroys and Christ Restores* (Greensboro, NC: New Growth Press, 2015), 180.
7. Langberg, *Suffering and the Heart of God*, 153.
8. Douglas Kaine McKelvey, "A Liturgy for the Loss of a Child," in *Every Moment Holy II: Death, Grief, and Hope* (Nashville: Rabbit Room Press, 2021), 194.

Chapter 5: Powerlessness

1. Andy Crouch, *Playing God: Redeeming the Gift of Power* (Downers Grove, IL: InterVarsity Press, 2013), 9.
2. Richard Lints, *Identity and Idolatry: The Image of God and Its Inversions* (Downers Grove, IL: InterVarsity Press, 2015), 35–36.
3. Timothy Keller, "Hope, Race and Power—Timothy Keller [Sermon]," Gospel in Life, August 25, 2022, YouTube video, 35:07, https://www.youtube.com/watch?app=desktop&v=pYV9FCS34eM.
4. Mike Cosper, "The True Meaning of Being Made in God's Image," October 30, 2020, in *TGC Podcast*, produced by the Gospel Coalition, podcast, MP3 audio, 56:17, https://www.thegospelcoalition.org/podcasts/tgc-podcast/the-true-meaning-of-being-made-in-gods-image/.
5. Tony Reinke, "The Nail in the Coffin of Our Hearts," Desiring God, October 1, 2017, https://www.desiringgod.org/articles/the-nail-in-the-coffin-of-our-hearts.
6. Viktor E. Frankl, *Man's Search for Meaning* (Boston, MA: Beacon Press, 2015), x.
7. Reinhold Niebuhr, "Prayer for Serenity," Celebrate Recovery, accessed May 2, 2023, https://www.celebraterecovery.com/resources/serenity-prayer.

Chapter 6: Intimacy

1. Philip Yancey, *Reaching for the Invisible God: What Can We Expect to Find?* (Grand Rapids, MI: Zondervan, 2000), 121.
2. Elisabeth Elliot, *Suffering Is Never for Nothing* (Nashville: B&H Publishing Group, 2019), 44.
3. Ligon Duncan, *When Pain Is Real and God Seems Silent: Finding Hope in the Psalms* (Wheaton, IL: Crossway, 2020), 25.
4. Jerry Sittser, *A Grace Disguised: How a Soul Grows Through Loss*, revised and expanded ed. (Grand Rapids, MI: Zondervan, 2021), 56.
5. Matt Chandler, "Arrogance/Humility," The Village Church, May 3, 2015, video transcript, https://www.thevillagechurch.net/resources/sermons/arrogance-humility.

Chapter 7: Prayer

1. Jackie Hill Perry, *Holier Than Thou: How God's Holiness Helps Us Trust Him* (Nashville: B&H Publishing Group, 2021), 2.
2. Mark Vroegop, *Dark Clouds, Deep Mercy: Discovering the Grace of Lament* (Wheaton, IL: Crossway, 2019), 37.
3. Timothy Keller, *Prayer: Experiencing Awe and Intimacy with God* (New York: Penguin Books, 2014).
4. C. S. Lewis, *The Lion, the Witch and the Wardrobe* (1948; repr., New York: HarperCollins Publishers, 1998), 39.
5. Lindy Johnson has attachment resources and online workshops at her website: https://www.lindygreenjohnson.com.

Chapter 8: Hope

1. Ligon Duncan, *When Pain Is Real and God Seems Silent: Finding Hope in the Psalms* (Wheaton, IL: Crossway, 2020), 52.
2. Lysa TerKeurst, *It's Not Supposed to Be This Way: Finding Unexpected Strength When Disappointments Leave You Shattered* (Nashville: Thomas Nelson, 2018), 48.
3. Orlando Saer, *Big God: How to Approach Suffering, Spread the Gospel, Make Decisions, and Pray in the Light of a God Who Really Is in the Driving Seat of the World*, rev. ed. (Fearn, Ross-shire: Christian Focus, 2014), 71.
4. Tony Evans et al., *Divine Disruption: Holding on to Faith When Life Breaks Your Heart* (Nashville: Thomas Nelson, 2021), 150.

Chapter 10: Perspective

1. *State of the Bible 2023*, American Bible Society, accessed May 4, 2023, PDF, https://sotb.research.bible.
2. *State of the Bible 2023*, x.
3. Matt Capps, "Why Theology Matters," Lifeway Research, August 3, 2015, https://research.lifeway.com/2015/08/03/why-theology-matters/.
4. Ligonier Ministries, *Ligonier State of Theology 2022*, Lifeway Research, September 2022, PDF, https://research.lifeway.com/wp-content/uploads/2022/09/Ligonier-State-of-Theology-2022-Full-Report.pdf.
5. Gregory A. Smith, "About Three-in-Ten U.S. Adults Are Now Religiously Unaffiliated," Pew Research Center, December 14,

2021, https://www.pewresearch.org/religion/2021/12/14/about-three-in-ten-u-s-adults-are-now-religiously-unaffiliated/; Jeffrey M. Jones, "How Religious Are Americans?," Gallup, December 23, 2021, https://news.gallup.com/poll/358364/religious-americans.aspx.

6. "How U.S. Religion Composition Has Changed in Recent Decades," Pew Research Center, September 13, 2022, https://www.pewresearch.org/religion/2022/09/13/how-u-s-religious-composition-has-changed-in-recent-decades/.
7. *Strong's Greek Concordance*, s.v. "3126. mamónas," BibleHub, accessed May 4, 2023, https://biblehub.com/greek/3126.htm.
8. Augustine of Hippo, *Confessions*, 1, 1.5, archived on The Holy See, accessed May 4, 2023, https://www.vatican.va/spirit/documents/spirit_20020821_agostino_en.html.
9. David Green and Bill High, *Leadership Not by the Book: 12 Unconventional Principles to Drive Incredible Results* (Grand Rapids, MI: Baker Books, 2022), 22.
10. Dane C. Ortlund, *Gently and Lowly: The Heart of Christ for Sinners and Sufferers* (Wheaton, IL: Crossway, 2020), 151.

Chapter 11: Perseverance

1. C. S. Lewis, *A Grief Observed* (1961; repr., San Francisco: HarperSanFrancisco, 1989), 69.
2. William Bridges, *The Way of Transition: Embracing Life's Most Difficult Moments* (Cambridge, MA: Da Capo Press, 2001), 3.
3. "What Do Americans Believe About Jesus? 5 Popular Beliefs," Barna, April 1, 2015, https://www.barna.com/research/what-do-americans-believe-about-jesus-5-popular-beliefs/.
4. Jerry Bridges, *Trusting God* (Colorado Springs: NavPress, 2017), 173.
5. David Powlison, *God's Grace in Your Suffering* (Wheaton, IL: Crossway, 2018), 16.

Conclusion

1. Diane Langberg, *Suffering and the Heart of God: How Trauma Destroys and Christ Restores* (Greensboro, NC: New Growth Press, 2015), 64.

ABOUT THE AUTHORS

Michael McAfee is the president and founder of Inspire Experiences, a PhD student studying public theology at Southern Baptist Theological Seminary, and an Oklahoma City Thunder fanatic. His greatest accomplishment in life is escaping the friend zone with Lauren when they were in high school. Michael and Lauren wrote a book on next-gen Bible engagement titled *Not What You Think*. They are covenant members of Council Road Baptist Church where Michael serves as one of the teaching pastors.

Lauren McAfee is the founder and visionary of Stand for Life and also serves as the ministry director at Hobby Lobby. Lauren is the author of *Only One Life*, *Not What You Think*, *Legacy Study*, and *Created in the Image of God*. She is currently pursuing a PhD in Ethics and Policy. Lauren previously worked for her father, Steve Green, while he founded Museum of the Bible in Washington, DC, serving as curator, artifact collection manager, and director of community engagement. Lauren and Michael are happily married with two fierce and feminine girls, Zion and Zara.